THE KIDS' WORLD ALMANAC OF MUSIC

THE KIDS' WORLD ALMANAC OF MUSIC

MUSIC

From Rock to Bach

by **ELYSE SOMMER**

Illustrated by **JOHN LANE**

WORLD ALMANAC

AN IMPRINT OF PHAROS BOOKS • A SCRIPPS HOWARD COMPANY
NEW YORK

Cover illustration by Mark Teague
Cover design by Charles Kreloff
Interior design by Janet Tingey
Interior illustrations by John Lane

First published in 1992.

Library of Congress Cataloging-in-Publication Data
Sommer, Elyse.
    The kids world almanac of music : from rock to Bach
/ Elyse Sommer ; illustrated by John Lane.
        p.   cm.
    Includes index.
    Summary: Explores the world of music, its history, origins,
instruments, and terminology.
        ISBN 0-88687-522-6 (hc). — ISBN 0-88687-521-8 (pb)
        1. Music—Miscellanea—Juvenile literature. [1. Music.]
I. Lane, John, 1932–   ill. II. Title.
ML3928.S65   1992
780—dc20   91-28372   CIP   AC MN

Pharos Books are available at special discounts on bulk purchases for sales
promotions, premiums, fundraising or educational use. For details, contact the
Special Sales Department, Pharos Books, 200 Park Avenue, New York, NY
10166

Printed in the United States of America

World Almanac
An Imprint of Pharos Books
A Scripps Howard Company
200 Park Avenue
New York, N.Y. 10166

10   9   8   7   6   5   4   3   2   1

CONTENTS

INTRODUCTION AND ACKNOWLEDGMENTS

Here it is, music fans—a collection of interesting information and trivia about all kinds of music. It includes tons of facts about the top singles, albums, videos, and hits from movies and musicals, plus miniprofiles and intriguing odds and ends about famous musicians, as well as tips on everything from choosing and buying an instrument to starting your own group—and even a music lover's video guide.

For easy fact-finding, check the index at the end of the book. There are also special symbols to help you quickly identify the type of information in a particular section. Here's what they mean.

This introduces facts about famous people.

Here's your key to miscellaneous musical facts.

Look for this, if you're looking for information about inventions and inventors.

The star symbol is, not surprisingly, your key to facts about stars of the musical world.

Here's the symbol that precedes facts about groups and playing in a group.

Stop for this to find out more about music festivals and awards.

Slow down when you see this, if you want information about top-selling songs, albums, money-making jobs and other money matters.

The music calendar towards the end of the book has its own symbols to flag firsts, birthdays and events.

To give credit where credit is due, let's give a round of applause to the band of music enthusiasts whose comments and suggestions were invaluable in making final choices about the most fun and interesting facts for this book. Here's a big hand for Barbara Drake, editor of *Music Alive*, and Ellen S. Pollen and Diana B. Feld, who shared so much of their musical wit and wisdom. Many thanks also to the following: Jeff Sapan, of ASCAP; Phillip Caggiano, of the Metropolitan Opera Association; Sonja D. Lewis, of the Girl Scouts of the U.S.A.; Susan Teplinsky, of the Boy Scouts of America; Barbara Elleman, of the American Library Association; Christine Erb and Steve Satullo, of the Either/Or Bookstore in Pittsfield, Mass.; Dr. Merrill Goodman, of Otolaryngology Associates, and all the wonderful folks at the Tanglewood Music Center.

Last, but by no means least, is a big kiss and a hug to our terrific panel of kid consultants: Nancy Amstel, Stacy Robin Beck, David Best, Michael David Kass, Lauren M. Lang, Melody Ment, Joanne Rich, and Enid Stanton.

THE KIDS' WORLD ALMANAC
OF MUSIC

MUSIC YESTERDAY AND TODAY

Music is one of the oldest forms of human expression, even older than language. But it isn't something that just happens. Cavemen's primitive songs and drumbeats were their musical responses to a world without any sort of communications systems. Then as people's lives became more civilized music changed and developed along with the customs and styles of the day. In other words, no musical style exists in a vacuum. Each is connected to the times during which its composers lived. So fasten your seat belts and take a musical trip through time.

SOME ANCIENT HISTORY

- Our first evidence that music played an important part in ancient civilizations comes from the stone carvings and instruments of Egyptians who lived five thousand years ago.
- Our most gifted musical ancestors were the ancient Greeks. They were the first people to combine singing and drama and to invent a system for writing down music.

- The next major musical innovators were all associated with the churches established during early Christian times. They perfected the musical notation system that's still in use today and set up the first formal music schools.
- The most famous composer of early religious music was Giovanni Pierluigi da Palestrina (1526?–1594). As the man in charge of the singers at the famous Sistine Chapel in Rome, he had the best music job available in those days.

THE GREAT COMPOSERS HALL OF FAME

A Quintet of Musical Giants

The music written by the first two composers of the five you will meet here is full of showy sounds. This ornateness was very much in keeping with the elaborate details on the buildings and furniture of the period. Other great composers who lived during this *baroque* period included Claudio Monteverdi (1567–1643), Alessandro Scarlatti (1659–1725), Jean Baptiste Lully (1632–1687), Antonio Vivaldi (1678–1741), and Henry Purcell (1659–1695). The composers below are known as the *classical* composers. Their music, like the art of the period, was simpler than that of the baroque composers. It was also more lyrical.

Johann Sebastian Bach (1685–1750)

Johann Sebastian Bach became the most famous member of a large German musical family. His home was filled with music and children: twenty kids, five claviers (early pianos), and assorted stringed instruments. Papa Bach gave lessons to everyone in the family and wrote many keyboard pieces, especially for his home-grown orchestra. During Bach's life he was known mostly as an organist, not a composer. Today his work is considered so important that the time when he lived is often called the Age of Bach. One of his best-known compositions for the orchestra is the Brandenburg Concerto no. 5.

George Frederick Handel (1685–1759)

Handel and Bach had a lot in common. They were born in the same country in the same year. Both were organists and composers. But that's where the resemblance ends. Bach led a quiet life in Germany. Handel moved to England, where the British royal family soon depended on him to compose special music for their parties and fashionable events. When King George II decided to give a party on his royal barge (a flat-bottomed boat), Handel wrote his famous "Water Music" for the occasion. He performed it, along with a band of musicians, from a barge that sailed alongside the one carrying the royal family. His masterpiece the *Messiah* remains a Christmas hit.

Joseph Haydn (1732–1809)

The man often called the father of the modern symphony spent most of his career working for a rich Austrian prince. His job included conducting an orchestra, composing music, and handling all the details that go with running a music organization. One of his 125 symphonies became known as the *Surprise Symphony*. Haydn's boss, the prince, had a habit of catching a few Zs during a performance, so Haydn added a loud wake-up chord to this piece.

Wolfgang Amadeus Mozart (1756–1791)

Mozart began composing before most kids go to kindergarten. By the time he was six he had played the piano and violin in public. A year later, his father toured him and his sister (also a talented pianist) all over Europe. They played for the Empress of Austria and many other VIPs. The children's earnings enabled the Mozarts to buy their own carriage. However, they still had to face such eighteenth-century travel discomforts and dangers as bumpy roads and highway robbers. Fortunately, Mozart was not just a child wonder but a true genius who left the world a treasure trove of beautiful music, including operas like *The Magic Flute*. In 1991, to celebrate the two-hundredth anniversary of Mozart's death, all the theaters and organizations that make up New York's Lincoln Center launched a marathon two-year-long performance schedule of all his eight hundred works. That's a lot of Mozart, but then there are a lot of Mozart fans.

Ludwig van Beethoven (1770–1827)

When Beethoven first performed his Symphony no. 9 he was so deaf he could hear neither the thunder of the music nor the thunderous applause. The symphony's last section, "Ode to Joy," has found its way into church hymns and pop group recordings, and in 1989 it was played to celebrate the fall of the Berlin Wall in Germany. Once Beethoven even hit the pop charts. That was when Walter Murphy recorded a disco-rock version of his Fifth Symphony. It was called "A Fifth of Beethoven" and stayed on the charts for five months.

★ Backstage Anecdotes about the First Superstars

Pops Goes the "Old Whig"

Bach's fellow musicians, and even his musician sons, nick-named him the Old Whig, because they felt his music was old-fashioned. However, modern musicians have found many ways to say "not so." Here are a few examples:

- "A Lover's Concerto," adapted from Bach's "Minuet in G," was a top hit for the Toys in 1965 and for the Apollo 100 in 1972.
- The Modern Jazz Quartet's "Blues on Bach" is a jazz lover's favorite.
- In an album called "Bach Meets Rodgers and Hammer-stein," pianist John Arn imagines how Bach would have written a modern musical, and what modern musical composers would sound like writing in Bach's style.
- There's even an album called "Switched-On Bach," in which the Brandenburg Concerto and other works are played on Moog synthesizers.

Haydn and His Barber

A friend once visited Joseph Haydn while he was shaving. As the composer struggled with his blade he exclaimed, "I'd give my best quartet for a good razor." His friend rushed out and bought him a fine set of razors. Haydn, true to his word, gave him the quartet that became known as the "Razor's Quartet."

The Bang-up Beginning of Handel's "Music for the Royal Fireworks"

Handel wrote his "Music for the Royal Fireworks" for a real fireworks celebration at the English royal palace. The music got off with a big bang, but not quite the kind Handel had in mind. What happened was that the fireworks box blew up just as the music was about to begin. That was the end of the fireworks—but not of the music, which remains one of Handel's biggest hits.

Wonderful, Wacky Mozart

Mozart loved games. Sometimes he even composed with a pen in one hand and a billiard cue in the other. He also daydreamed a lot—so much, in fact, that his wife had to cut his meat for him, so he wouldn't absentmindedly slice off a finger.

Beethoven: Klutz and Oddball

Although Beethoven wasn't clumsy when his fingers hit the piano, he was forever dropping dishes, breaking vases, and bumping into furniture. He also had an odd habit of letting cold water pour over his hands before he sat down to compose. He said it helped him to think.

Musical Romantics and Patriots

During the 1800s and early 1900s all the arts were what we call *romantic*. Piano and violin performances were filled with grand, emotional passages, and audiences went absolutely crazy over grand opera. Another term used to describe many composers of this period is that they were nationalistic. Many used their talents to whip up national pride by building the flavor of their country's legends and folk songs into their music. This section tells you about some of the best known of the many talented musicians who created beautiful romantic and nationalistic music.

Franz Peter Schubert (1797–1828)

Germans call art songs lieder; Franz Schubert was one of Germany's leading lieder composers. He was so full of melodies that when paper wasn't handy he often wrote his beautiful tunes on tablecloths, napkins, or shirt cuffs. He published the first of his six hundred songs when he was just fifteen. It was called "The Erlking," and was about a father trying to save his sick child from being snatched by death. Sad to say, Schubert himself was snatched away early by death, when he was just thirty-one years old.

Felix Mendelssohn (1809–1847)

Because Mendelssohn was playing the piano in public by the time he was nine he was often compared to Mozart. However, unlike Mozart he had a normal and happy childhood. In fact, Mendelssohn was one of the few composers who was born with a "silver spoon in his mouth" and never had to struggle to make a living. His famous overture to Shakespeare's play *A Midsummer Night's Dream* was composed when Mendelssohn was seventeen. Part of this has become a much-played wedding march.

Frederic Chopin (1810–1849)

Chopin left his native Poland to work in France, but the music he wrote was inspired by his home country, especially its formal dance, the polonaise. Piano students everywhere continue to love and play his music. It's also been used in movies, and a jazzed-up version of his "Fantaisie Impromptu" became a pop hit called "I'm Always Chasing Rainbows."

Franz Liszt (1811–1886)

Liszt is another in a long line of child wonders. He was an outstanding pianist at seven, composed at eight, and made concert appearances at nine. As an adult, Liszt was a true international superstar. Women were wild about his elegant profile, so to give them the best possible view Liszt had the piano placed sideways. This position eventually became a standard for all concert pianists, no matter what their profiles were like. Liszt traveled all over the map, but his beautiful Hungarian Rhapsodies prove that he never forgot his own country.

Richard Wagner (1813–1883)
You probably know more of this composer's work than you think. His opera *Lohengrin* contains a wedding march known to many people as "Here Comes the Bride." In addition, many cartoon shows and movies have used bits and pieces from his other operas. Although Wagner disliked many people, he loved animals and kept ten dogs around the house. He considered no tune finished until the one he called Peps gave it a bark of approval.

Giuseppe Verdi (1813–1901)
Verdi was the fastest as well as the most popular opera composer in the world. *Rigoletto, Il Trovatore,* and *La Traviata* were all written within the same three years.

Johannes Brahms (1833–1897)
Brahms's father discouraged his interest in music, but an older composer named Robert Schumann recognized his genius and gave him a helping hand toward becoming a successful musician. Brahms always kept his pockets filled with candy to give to any children he met. His work includes compositions for the orchestra, and his Hungarian Dances. His "Lullaby" has become as much a folk song as a classical composition.

Peter Ilyich Tchaikovsky (1840–1893)
This Russian composer's work includes several pieces loved by children all over the world: the beautiful ballet music for "The Nutcracker" and the rousing 1812 Overture. One of his pieces was rewritten as a hit song called "Tonight We Love."

Edvard Grieg (1843–1907)

The man whose music is said to best characterize the Norse spirit was actually born into a family of Scottish origin. The folk melodies that gave his music their national flavor were all original compositions. Grieg was probably one of the smallest composers who ever lived. The clothes in his closet looked more like a doll's than a great composer's. His lovely "Peer Gynt" suite is an enduring classical hit.

Ralph Vaughan Williams (1872–1958)

If you want to know what makes English music sound English, listen to some recordings of this composer's work. He often used actual English folk songs, as in the "Fantasia on 'Greensleeves.' "

Charles Ives (1874–1954)

This part-time songwriter (he ran a successful insurance company) was the first American composer to use the songs of his native land. In fact, he used a little of a lot of things, from jazz to hymns to country fiddlers' tunes. Ives not only borrowed popular tunes but often took them through some mighty peculiar variations. His takeoff on "America" in "Variations on a National Hymn" is a good example. He won a Pulitzer Prize for his Third Symphony, but not until forty years after he wrote it.

CATCHING THE TWENTIETH - CENTURY MUSICAL EXPRESS

The twentieth century is filled with exciting musical developments. Because no one seems to have come up with a better name, anything that's easy to sing or dance to is called *popular*. The music by the great composers of the past is called *classical*. The music of this century's classical composers is called *twentieth century, contemporary*, or *serious* music. The first two composers in this section had one foot in the nineteenth century and another in the twentieth. Their music introduced the idea of moving back and forth or crossing over from one style of music to another.

Claude Debussy (1862–1918)

This early starter from France was playing the piano and composing by the time he was twelve. Debussy is known as an *impressionistic* musician, because he tried to capture the mood of an action instead of the action itself. His famous "Clair de Lune," for example, creates the feeling of rippling water.

Maurice Ravel (1875–1937)

Early in his career Ravel composed some impressionistic music, as did his fellow countryman Debussy. His biggest hit, "Bolero," was written for the great ballet dancer Sergei Diaghilev. It's unique because it has a single melody, which is repeated over and over again, each time louder than before. There have been "Bolero" performances by every type of musical group from symphony orchestras to jazz bands.

Igor Stravinsky (1882–1971)

This twentieth-century style maker was also one of the first to direct, conduct, supervise, and play the piano for his recorded works. His best-known compositions were written for the ballet. Two that are particularly popular are "The Firebird," which is based on a legend of a prince who captures a fabulous Firebird and receives from it a magic feather; and "Petrushka," in which a lovable doll is brought to life.

Aaron Copland (1900–1990)

Copland's music often sounds and feels like American folk music. Although he used actual folk songs, he always changed them around to make them more interesting. One of his ballet compositions, "Appalachian Spring," won a Pulitzer Prize. Another was based on the story of the famous outlaw Billy the Kid. He also wrote lots of movie background music.

George Gershwin (1898–1937)

With his "American in Paris" and "Rhapsody in Blue," George Gershwin proved that jazz wasn't just "cutting loose" music but was powerful enough to combine well with symphonic music. His musical play *Porgy and Bess* has been produced as both a film and an opera.

Leonard Bernstein (1918–1990)

This composer, pianist, and conductor could be called one of the first classical-to-pop crossover superstars. He moved easily from the concert stage to Broadway and back. You probably know at least one song from his music for *West Side Story*, a popular stage and movie musical about two street gangs.

Phillip Glass (b. 1937)

Phillip Glass is an opera composer (*Einstein at the Beach*) whose music has also been played on television ("Sesame Street," "Saturday Night Live") and in the movies (*The Thin Blue Line*). He is one of a group of composers known as minimalists. Their music has less melody and more rocklike rhythms than other classical music styles. For another example of this composer's classical–pop connection, see the summary of rock in the 1980s in the section called "Rock's Most Memorable Moments," later in this chapter.

ROCK 'N' ROLL: A RIVER INTO WHICH MANY STREAMS FLOW

Rock 'n' roll is like a river with several streams of American musical sounds flowing into it. The river has now grown into a huge mainstream called *pop*. Here are some facts about the first waves of sound that streamed into the rock 'n' roll river.

The blues is an African-American type of folk song that dates back to the beginning of this century. When the blues spread from the rural areas of the South to the cities, its simple pattern of twelve beats (musical measures) became more intricate. In the 1930s the famous bandleader Count Basie added a jazzy, easy-to-dance-to sound to the blues. That was the beginning of *rhythm and blues*, or *R&B* for short.

Jazz began with a ragged dance beat called ragtime. This was especially popular in New Orleans during the early 1900s. After a while the ragtime bands broke up into small groups.

They played "hot," or with lots of feeling and freedom, plus the sound of the blues. This led to jazz, which brought the end of ragtime.

Gospel music was first heard in American churches during the days of slavery. In the late 1940s it drifted toward rock 'n' roll with a blind singer and pianist named Ray Charles. He blended it with a touch of the blues and pop into a new mix that became known as *soul music*. Aretha Franklin, Dionne Warwick, and Whitney Houston are just a few of the popular performers who started out as gospel singers in their church choirs.

Country music added another important element to rock music. It ranged from the twangy songs known as *hillbilly* to the scratchy guitars of the music known as *bluegrass*.

Pop was the name invented to describe smooth, easy-to-listen-to songs. Rock 'n' roll was a rebellion against this smooth sound, but even so, it has always contained a generous dash of pop. Today's tops-in-pops lists include singers like Mariah Carey, Michael Bolton, and many more.

ROCK'S MOST MEMORABLE MOMENTS

It's fun to look back over rock 'n' roll's long and colorful history—almost forty years of songs, styles, and style mixes to keep the beat going and growing! For a whirlwind tour of the sounds and sights unique to the rock 'n' roll decades from the 1950s to the 1990s, read on.

From Easy Listening to Elvis: The 1950s

The first half of the fifties was all pop, with no rock. The term *rock 'n' roll* didn't even exist until a disc jockey (a radio personality who selects and introduces recorded music) named Alan Freed invented it as a catchy name for his new rhythm-and-blues music show.

• Country or hillbilly singers developed their own brand of rhythm and blues. This became known as *rockabilly*.

- *Doo-wop* was another bouncy name and style of this period. Like rap music, it was born in the streets of big cities. Singing groups who couldn't afford instruments gathered on street corners and repeated silly words like "sha-na-na-na-na" to accompany their melodies.
- Two key events turned rock 'n' roll into a musical phenomenon: a song called "Rock Around the Clock," in a movie about a bunch of tough high school kids; and Elvis Presley's first shake, rattle, and roll appearance on national prime-time television. He was rock 'n' roll's first superstar.

Rock for All Ages: The 1960s

- This decade got off to a bouncy start with a brand-new dance called *the Twist,* introduced by Chubby Checker. Kids liked its catchy rhythm and the fact that you could do it either with or without a partner.
- Teenaged rock fans got their very own show, "American Bandstand." Many teen stars got their start on this 1960s-style "Club MTV". It also popularized many other rock dances, like the *Bop, Limbo, Locomotion, Slop, Swim, Stroll, Calypso, Frug, Mashed potato, Watusi*, and *Chicken*.
- The sixties wouldn't have been the sixties without female groups like the Ronettes, the Shirelles, and the Supremes. Unlike many of today's groups, they didn't write their own music or play their own instruments. That meant they had less control over their performances.
- During this period rock 'n' roll went international. This happened when four talented and original English musicians who called themselves the Beatles became a supergroup.
- Rock also spread its appeal to older audiences. A new style called *folk rock* had a lot to do with this. It combined folk melodies, pop, and the blues into songs with more serious subjects. Some of folk rock's biggest stars were Bob Dylan, Joan Baez, and the group Peter, Paul, and Mary.

Mixing It Up and Making It Louder: The 1970s

- The Beatles' use of Indian instruments in some of their songs inspired other combinations of rock and nonrock music (for example, rock and jazz). This was known as *fusion* or *crossover* music. The Grammy Award–winning electronic keyboard musician Chick Corea successfully expanded this idea when he mixed jazz with classical and Brazilian music.
- A bunch of new English bands began to play music that sounded as tough and angry as they looked. This *punk rock* was even louder than today's heavy metal music.
- Rock dances had lots of breaking, popping, and locking.
- The seventies also brought the first family superkid group to rock, the Jackson Five.

New Sounds, New Mergers, News a'Plenty: The 1980s

- A new electronic instrument, the synthesizer, started to show up on the rock bandstand in the eighties.
- The boundaries between rock and nonrock styles continued to disappear. American rock combined with South African pop, Brazilian music, a rhythm and blues style from Jamaica called *reggae*, and *calypso* (remember "Under the Sea" from *The Little Mermaid*). Groups like Gloria Estefan and her Miami Sound Machine made a spicy mix of Cuban, jazz, rock, and rhythm and blues. There was even a new name for it all: *world beat*.
- Even the line separating classical or "serious" from pop musicians began to stretch. When Phillip Glass, the minimalist composer, recorded a new work, "Songs from Liquid Days," he collaborated with popular songwriters Paul Simon, David Byrne, Laurie Anderson, and Suzanne Vega. Linda Ronstadt was also one of his performing artists.
- Sidestepping dances like the *smurf* and the *bird* were popular.

- *Rock videos*, a type of commercial for new records, turned into a brand-new entertainment form. And rock fans got a twenty-four-hour cable network called MTV, plus an update of "American Bandstand" called "Club MTV."
- Eighties kids loved *heavy metal* or *hard rock* bands as much as their parents hated them. For those with more quiet tastes there were also new singers accompanying themselves on nonelectric guitars (for example, Tracy Chapman and the Indigo Girls), and a jazzy new type of *a capella* (singing without instruments), by Bobby McFerrin.
- *Rap* burst onto the music scene. This combination of dancing, talking, and singing in rhyme wasn't really a brand-new style. It began in West African villages and on southern slave plantations and had been used by jazz musicians during the 1940s and 1950s. It was rappers with catchy names like L. L. Cool J and Run-D.M.C., who gave rap a new sound by mixing it with soul and heavy metal sounds.
- Fans who put new songs and stars on the maps got younger. For example, it was grade- and middle-school kids, not older teenagers, who helped the New Kids on the Block move off the block and up to the stars in 1989.
- The year 1989 also had a lot of "old rock" news, especially reunion tours by rockers whose music was popular in the sixties and seventies, like the Rolling Stones and Paul McCartney.
- The new young stars were very much "say no to drugs" types, and most of the older rockers traded in their bad habits for family lives and health food.

The More Things Change: The 1990s

- Just four months into 1990, Bonnie Raitt, Paula Abdul, Janet Jackson, Allanah Myles, Lisa Stansfield, and Sinead O'Connor had best-selling albums. Female superstars were definitely in!
- The nineties also rolled on with lots of *rap 'n rock* and more international-style mixes. Singer-songwriter Paul Simon, who was the first to combine rock, African, and

Brazilian music ("Graceland," 1986) did it again with "The Rhythm of the Saints."

- Early rock styles showed up on many new recordings. For example, Marvin Gaye, a rock legend of the seventies, influenced both Terence Trent D'Arby's album "Neither Fish Nor Flesh" and M. C. Hammer's "Please Hammer Don't Hurt 'Em."

- Television's favorite family, the Simpsons, hopped onto the musical trail. The star of their top-selling music video, "The Simpsons Sing the Blues," was, of course, Bart.

- Kids and their parents took to line dancing, especially the *electric slide*. No partner needed!

- Like the folk rock songs of the 1970s, many new songs appealed to the listeners' social conscience, such as "Another Day in Paradise," by Phil Collins.

- All the highlights from all of rock's decades add up to the fact that musical styles are not easy to put into one slot. As new sounds borrow from the old, the only thing that's clear to see is that the more things change, the more they remain the same. And no matter how many new musical streams come along, the rock 'n' roll river can absorb them all.

ROLLING INTO THE NINETIES WITH THE TOP OF THE POPS

Only a few of the names on best-of-the-year lists end up on the best-of-the-decade lists. Which of these 1990s stars do you think will make it to the round-up lists at the end of the century? (Check out Chapter 5 for the 1990 Grammy Awards, and Chapter 9 for chart toppers in other categories.)

Billboard's List of the Ten Top Pop Singles for 1990

1. "Hold On." Wilson Phillips.
2. "It Must Have Been Love" (from *Pretty Woman*). Roxette.
3. "Nothing Compares To U." Sinead O'Connor.
4. "Poison." Bell Biv DeVoe.

5. "Vogue." Madonna.
6. "Vision of Love." Mariah Carey.
7. "Another Day in Paradise." Phil Collins.
8. "Hold On." En Vogue.
9. "Cradle of Love" (from *Ford Fairlane*). Billy Idol.
10. "Blaze of Glory" (from *Young Guns II*). Jon Bon Jovi.

Billboard's List of the Ten Top Pop Albums for 1990

1. "Rhythm Nation 1814." Janet Jackson.
2. ". . .But Seriously." Phil Collins.
3. "Soul Provider." Michael Bolton.
4. "Pump." Aerosmith.
5. "Please Hammer Don't Hurt 'Em." M. C. Hammer.
6. "Forever Your Girl." Paula Abdul.
7. "Dr. Feelgood." Motley Crue.
8. "The End of the Innocence." Don Henley.
9. "Cosmic Thing." B-52's.
10. "Storm Front." Billy Joel.

MTV'S Ten Top Music Videos for 1990

The titles in parentheses give the albums from which the videos were made.

1. M. C. Hammer. "U Can't Touch This" ("Please Hammer Don't Hurt 'Em").
2. Billy Idol. "Cradle of Love" ("Charmed Life").
3. Madonna. "Vogue" ("I'm Breathless").
4. Aerosmith. "Janie's Got a Gun" ("Pump").
5. Paula Abdul. "Opposites Attract" ("Forever Your Girl").
6. Sinead O'Connor. "Nothing Compares To U" ("I Do Not Want What I Haven't Got").
7. Vanilla Ice. "Ice Ice Baby" ("To the Extreme").
8. Jon Bon Jovi. "Blaze of Glory" ("Young Gun II").
9. Janet Jackson. "Escapade" ("Rhythm Nation 1814").
10. Motley Crue. "Don't Go Away Mad . . . (Just Go Away)" ("Dr. Feelgood").

MUSIC GOES 'ROUND THE WORLD

In their entire lifetimes, Mozart and other musical greats never had audiences as large as those for a single modern concert or record. Jet travel, improved recording methods, and television have produced a true musical global village with an international music menu.

AN ALL-STAR INTERNATIONAL CAST FROM ALL WALKS OF MUSIC

Name	Type of Musician	Native Country
Paula Abdul	Pop singer–dancer	United States
Phil Collins	Pop singer–songwriter	England
Placido Domingo	Opera singer	Mexico
k.d. Lang	Country music–pop singer	Canada
Zubin Mehta	Classical conductor	India
Midori	Classical violinist	Japan
Sinead O'Connor	Pop singer–songwriter	Ireland
Luciano Pavarotti	Opera singer	Italy

GROUPS AROUND THE GLOBE

Group Name	Type of Music	Native Country
a-ha	Rock trio	Norway
Aquarium	Folk rock	Russia
Canadian Brass	Five-piece group dedicated to proving that classical music can be fun	Canada
The Chieftains	Folk music	Ireland
Gorky Park	Hard rock	Russia
Roxette	Pop-rock	Sweden
Fine Young Cannibals	Pop-rock	England

GROUPS AROUND THE GLOBE

Group Name	Type of Music	Native Country
Jeff Healey Band	Blues-rock	Canada
Inxs (pronounced "in excess")	Pop-rock	Australia
Kassav	Zouk rhythms	Guadeloupe
Nelson	Rock duo	United States
Savuka	Zulu dance music	South Africa
Simple Minds	Rock sextet	Scotland
Scorpions	Rock group	West Germany

DANCIN' AROUND THE WORLD

Country	Dance Name and Description
Argentina	Tango: Stylish dance with lots of turns and dips.
Austria	Waltz: Graceful partner dance.
Bohemia	Polka: Fast-moving folk dance that sounds Polish but isn't.
Brazil	Samba: Happy, bouncy dance done to a drum sound.
Cuba	Conga: Group dance with a one-two-three-kick pattern.
	Mambo: Combination Latin and jazz dance.
	Rhumba: Jazzy partner dance.
Czechoslovakia	Dunka: folk dance.
Hungary	Czardas: Slow-starting dance that turns wild and exciting in the second part.
Ireland	Jigs, reels: Step dances done to the accompaniment of various instruments.
Israel	Hora: Dancers join hands to form large circle, moving around with steps and kicks.
Italy	Tarantella: Lively courtship dance with lots of improvisation that goes back to 200 B.C.
Mexico	La Raspa: Folk dance performed with a shuffling step that sounds a little like the rasping sound of a file.

DANCIN' AROUND THE WORLD

Country	Dance Name and Description
Peru	Echunga Para La Yunga: Circle dance.
Philippines	Tinikling: Fast dance with bamboo sticks; named for a bird that looks like a crane.
Russia	Troika: Square dance.
Spain	Flamenco: Foot-stomping dance of the Spanish gypsies.
South Africa	Umzani: Type of Zulu war dancing made internationally famous by Johnny Clegg and his band, Savuka.
United States	Rap Dancing: Acrobatic dances that started with Breakdancing, the Electric boogie, and the Moonwalk.

Music for a Better World

It's true that some rock musicians have gotten themselves into some bad situations. But there's another side to this image that's illustrated by their many spectacularly successful projects on behalf of worthy causes.

Nobody's Child.　This was the first big benefit album of the 1990s. The lead song was by the Traveling Wilburys. Other songs were donated by stars like Stevie Wonder, Billy Idol, Eric Clapton, and the Bee Gees. The money raised went to Romanian orphans.

Farm-Aid 1990.　This annual event began in 1985 when folk singer Bob Dylan came up with the idea for a concert to raise money for America's farmers. The 1990 concert featured its usual bumper crop of stars and raised $1.3 million. It ended with the all-star cast singing "This Land Is Your Land."

Red, Hot & Blue.　This benefit album featured Cole Porter

songs sung by Sinead O'Connor, David Byrne, the Neville Brothers, k. d. Lang, Neneh Cherry, and Fine Young Cannibals. It was televised on International Aids Day in October 1990.

Rain-forest Action Benefits.   Special benefits were organized to preserve the rain forests that are so important to a healthy world environment. One of these, in 1989, was a world fund-raising tour by Sting and the chief of a Brazilian Indian tribe.

Our Common Future.   This spectacular musical "wake-up call to save our planet" featured superstar performances in Rio, Moscow, Tokyo, and Sydney. It was televised in 1989 to more than 100 countries.

The Moscow Peace Music Festival.   Before the new openness, or *glasnost* in Soviet society that began in 1989, this festival couldn't have happened. The two-day concert brought together U.S. and Soviet Union groups on a 186-by-120-foot stage at Lenin Stadium in Moscow. All the profits were donated to antidrug organizations in both countries.

The Human Rights Now Tour.   This six-week, 35,000-mile global celebration in 1988 was inspired by the fortieth anniversary of the UN Universal Declaration of Human Rights. Bruce Springsteen, Sting, Peter Gabriel, and Tracy Chapman were some of the stars who contributed their talents.

Live-Aid.   This concert combined the spirit of Band-Aid (see below) and USA (see below) into two seventeen-hour-long concerts telecast in 1985 from Wembley Stadium in London and the John F. Kennedy Stadium in Philadelphia. This event raised millions of dollars for the people of East Africa and continues to inspire other benefit efforts.

Band-Aid.   This catchy name was used by a group of English musicians to record the first pop tune written especially to raise money for charity. They recorded "Do They Know It's

Christmas" in December 1984. By the following Christmas, it had earned $11 million for famine-relief organizations working in Ethiopia and the Sudan.

USA (United Support of Artists) for Africa. This American version of Band-Aid recorded "We Are the World" in 1985. The song became an anthem of good will for the rest of the decade.

The Bangladesh Concert. This concert, organized in 1971 by ex-Beatle George Harrison, was the first superevent to help the needy. More than 20,000 people came to hear stars from both sides of the Atlantic sing and play. They raised more than $15 million to send to starving people in war-torn Bangladesh.

INVENTIONS THAT HAVE MADE TODAY'S KIDS THE MOST MUSICAL EVER

Want to hear what made the great composers great? Just turn on the radio, borrow a cassette or CD from your library, and listen up. It's all possible because of the work done by some of the people described below. Some truly awesome new listening advances already in the works include a system to compress sound so that practically all the recorded music ever made can be stored on a single computer disc!

Invention: Compact Disc.
Inventor: The Phillips Company.
Year: 1982.

Digital recordings are the latest step toward the most accurate and permanent possible sound reproduction. In these recordings sound is picked up from a plastic surface with a tiny laser. People started to accept compact discs shortly after the Dire Straits' "Brothers in Arms" sold over a million copies in 1986.

Invention: Transistor.
Inventors: John Bardeen, Walter Brattain, William Shockley.
Year: 1947.

The portable radio as well as sound and recording equipment are the result of these three physicists' search for a smaller and more energy-efficient substitute for the electron tube. The word *transistor* is a combination of the words transfer and resistor. True to its name, a transistor regulates the flow of electric current, through a combination of conductivity and resistance.

Invention: Stereo/multichannel recording.
Inventor: A. D. Blumlein.
Year: 1931.

The development of stereo made listening to recorded music more than just second-best to hearing it live. Walt Disney's famous movie *Fantasia* was the first one with a stereo soundtrack.

Invention: Dynamic loudspeaker.
Inventors: Charles W. Rice, Edward W. Kellogg.
Year: 1924.

At one time people needed hard headphones to listen to the radio and an acoustical (nonelectric) horn for their record players. But once these two engineers developed a loudspeaker with a moving coil, such cumbersome equipment was no longer necessary.

Invention: Video disc.
Inventor: John Logie Baird.
Year: 1924.

John Logie Baird began his experiments with transmitting pictures by radio waves and sound with a cardboard disc cut from a hatbox and a projection lamp housed in an empty cookie tin. This gave him the idea to develop a wax-coated cardboard disc that revolved at high speed and contained about a minute's worth of a very blurry picture. Then almost fifty years passed before researchers for two European electronics companies came up with a similar idea. Their disc could record pictures in full color as well as hold longer-playing sound.

Invention: Tape recorder.
Inventors: Valdemar Poulsen, Fritz Pfleumer, George Eash.
Years: 1898—1954.

This three-step invention began with a wire recorder by Poulsen in 1898. Next came Pfleumer's development of magnetic tape in 1932. Eash's tape cartridge, developed in 1954, was step three.

Invention: Phonograph record.
Inventors: Thomas Edison, Charles Cros, Emile Berliner, Peter Goldmark.
Years: 1877—1957.

Edison built the first phonograph, but a Frenchman named Charles Cros actually described it first. Emile Berliner improved on the Edison-Cros invention. Peter Goldmark then perfected Berliner's improvements and gave us the long-playing record. It took another thirty-eight years for the next step up this ladder of invention—the development of an electric model.

Invention: Broadcasting.
Inventors: Guglielmo Marconi, Lee De Forest, Edwin H. Armstrong.
Years: 1895—1939.

Experiments with electrical communications were considered the cat's whiskers in the 1890s. Marconi's system for sending wireless messages and De Forest's audio tube for sending messages by voice got radio broadcasting started. Then Major Edwin Armstrong improved the broadcast sound with FM stereo.

Invention: **Microphone.**
Inventor: **Thomas Edison.**
Year: **1877.**

Two men besides Edison who deserve credit for this invention were Alexander Graham Bell and Emile Berliner.

FAMOUS PEOPLE TRIVIA

2

If you love celebrity trivia, you're not alone. Here's a whole chapter of star trivia. You may know that Stan Kirk Burrell is really M. C. Hammer, but do you know how he got that name? You'll also discover what Wilson Phillips, the group that started to burn up the charts in 1990, has to do with the Beach Boys from the 1960s.

★ FASHION AND STYLE
Seven Ways Stars Dress for Success

Color, Glitter, and Glitz
Music is as much show as sound. M. C. Hammer's colorful, baggy pants and tops that glitter or show lots of Hammer skin are all part of his image. Perhaps his two thousand or so outfits will one day be in a museum like the one that holds the jeweled outfits and seventy-five-foot-long white fox cape once worn by the pianist Liberace.

Shock Appeal
Groups like Motley Crue are known for their metal-studded

clothes and heavy metal, tattoo-covered arms. It's the "bad boy" look that fans seem to expect from these hard-rocking groups. During the 1970s the group Kiss shocked and dazzled fans with their eerie makeup. Their fans never saw them "bare faced" until 1983. The result? No makeup, no hits!

Everything One Color
The singer-composer-producer Prince added to his royal image by using the color purple as his trademark. His song "Purple Rain" was a no. 2 hit for eleven weeks. And you can probably guess why the country music singer Johnny Cash became famous as the Man in Black.

Spiffy Shades
Elton John has had twenty years of hits, from "Goodbye Yellow Brick Road" to "I Don't Wanna Go On with You Like That." He no longer needs jeweled, feathered, and fur-trimmed eyeshades to get attention, but people sure noticed them when he started out. Buddy Holly, whose songs "That'll Be the Day" and "Peggy Sue" became early rock 'n' roll classics, was the first popular singer to wear ordinary glasses on stage. His no-frills, four-eyed look got him nicknamed the musical Clark Kent (superhero Superman's everyday name).

Something Missing
For most people a single glove means a lost glove. But when Michael Jackson made "Thriller" wearing just one glove, his reputation as an "original" zoomed. He then accumulated a whole wardrobe of single gloves. Some were embroidered with as many as 1,200 rhinestones and cost $5,000.

One Super Simple Prop
On the classical concert stage, tuxedos and simple gowns are the rule. But some stars manage to make a big deal out of something quite ordinary. Take the handkerchief most musicians keep handy but out of sight to wipe away sweat. Opera star Luciano Pavarotti never appears without a large white handkerchief in his hand. Vladimir Horowitz, the pianist who

topped the classical charts throughout his life, was known for his bow ties.

More Plain than Fancy

No fussy outfits, hairdos, and makeup for Canadian country singer k.d. Lang! Her clothes could have come right out of a barn, and she doesn't wear even a smidgen of makeup. Even the way she tucks her name, Kathy Dawn, into two lowercase initials is part of her image. It all adds up to "singer" instead of "female singer."

Some "Hairy" Tales

- The 1990 news about female singers' hair was no hair at all, at least for that leading lady of pop Sinead O'Connor.
- The B-52's, a 1960s group that hit the big time in 1990, named themselves after a 1960s women's hairdo. Their two female members always wear big bouffant "beehive" wigs.
- The dictionary doesn't have a listing for *rocker hair*, but if it did it might be long, free-flowing hair loaded with hair spray. Robert Smith of the Cure has one of the more outlandish "rockerheads" around.
- The man who styles the hair of the Bon Jovi rock group is leader Jon Bon Jovi's own dad. He's a professional hair dresser.
- Milli Vanilli's hair extensions cost $750 each and took eight hours to weave into place. They probably shopped around for something cheaper after losing their 1989 Grammy Award because they never actually sang "Girl You Know It's True."
- Multicolored hair dates back to the early rocker named Little Richard, who used to spray his hair silver.
- Long, flowing hairstyles were so common on the nineteenth-century concert stage that after a while all classical musicians were nicknamed "longhairs."
- Sometimes famous performers inspire a hairstyle. In the 1800s, barbers had many requests for haircuts "à la Capone," like the opera tenor Joseph Capone. But when the

real Capone once asked a barber for an "à la Capone" cut he was told, "Sorry, you don't have the head to carry that style"!

THE MUSICAL NAME GAME

Show-biz people have always dropped the names on their birth certificates for snappier, more memorable "handles." Here are a few that you may know.

NAME DROPPERS

Stage Name	*Real Name*
Kool (Kool and the Gang)	Robert Bell; birthday unknown
Pat Benatar	Pat Andrzejewsky; b. 1952
Elvis Costello	Declan McManus; b. August 25, 1955
John Denver	Henry John Deutschendorf, Jr.; b. December 31, 1943
Sheena Easton	Sheena Shirley Orr; b. April 27, 1959
Chaka Kahn	Yvette Marie Stevens; b. March 23, 1953
Cher	Cherilyn Sarkissian; b. May 20, 1946
Madonna	Madonna Louise Ciccone; b. January 16, 1958
Sade	Helen Folsade Adu; b. January 16, 1959
Tiffany	Tiffany Darwisch; b. October 2, 1971
Steven Tyler (Aerosmith)	Steven Tallarico; birthday unknown
Vanilla Ice	Robert Van Winkle; b. October 31, 1968
Bono Vox (U2)	Paul Hewson; birthday unknown

The Stories Behind Eight Famous Stage Names

Sting (Gordon Sumner, b. 1951)
This actor, singer, and guitarist used to wear a yellow and black rugby T-shirt. It made him look like a bee, and you know what a bee can do.

David Bowie (David Robert Jones, b. 1947)
This English pop star and actor's nickname was inspired by the long, single-bladed bowie knife used on the American frontier.

Meat Loaf (Marvin Lee Aday, b. 1947)
This rocker was Meat Loaf long before he became well known in the 1970s. His handle started in the seventh grade, when this singer was five feet two and weighed 240 pounds.

The Rolling Stones
Brian Jones, the Stones' guitarist, named the group after a song called "Rollin' Stone" written in 1950 by the legendary blues musician Muddy Waters.

Billy Idol (William Broad, b. 1941)
This British rock star took this name as a joke, because "no one could possibly take an idol seriously." He also says he once had a teacher who sent home a note saying that "William is idle."

Bob Dylan (Robert Allen Zimmerman, b. 1941)
This singer-songwriter-guitarist-harmonica player, who's been a superstar since 1965, named himself after the poet Dylan Thomas.

Bo Diddley (Ortho Ellas Bates McDaniel, b. 1928)
This influential singer-guitarist, who began recording in 1955 and was inducted into the Rock and Roll Hall of Fame in 1987, took his name from a kind of one-stringed African guitar.

Nellie Melba (Helen Mitchell, 1861–1931)
This opera singer toured all over the world. She took her stage name from her home city of Melbourne, Australia.

Nicknamed by Friends

The names in the list above were chosen by the stars themselves. The labels below were made up by fellow musicians, friends, or fans.

Joan Baez: The Nonviolent Singer (b. 1941)
This name originated during the 1960s when this folksinger sang at many protest and peace movement rallies.

Willie Nelson: The Shakespeare of Country Music (b. 1933)
Willie Nelson writes songs almost as fast as William Shakespeare wrote plays. His output to date comes to more than two thousand songs.

Chet Atkins: Mr. Nashville (b. 1920)
This guitar player was country instrumentalist of the year five times in the fifteen years between 1967 and 1982. His nametag honors his many efforts to promote other Nashville musicians.

Franco Corelli: The Bad Boy of Opera (b. 1923)
If the modern opera world had a Hall of Shame, Franco Corelli might be in it for his fiery temperament. Once he got so angry at a soprano for trying to hog the limelight that he bit her. She outlasted him on a high note.

Louis Armstrong: Satchmo (1900–1971)
Satchmo is a contraction of "satchel mouth," which describes the shape of this great jazz trumpeter's mouth. His name became a household word in 1965 when he made his no. 1 recording of "Hello Dolly!"

Carl Sandburg: The Old Troubadour (1878–1967)
When Sandburg was a struggling young poet, he worked as a professional folksinger and guitar player to help support his family. The troubadour tag was given to him by another famous man, architect Frank Lloyd Wright.

Elizabeth Taylor Greenfield: The Black Swan (1809–1876)
Greenfield was born into slavery and raised by a Philadelphia family. Her adopted mother recognized her talent and paid for her voice training. The black swan label followed her throughout a concert career that took her all over the United States and to England, where she performed for Queen Victoria.

George Frederick Handel: The Thunderbolt (1685–1759)
This tag was given by one great composer to another. Mozart, who was no slowpoke himself, tagged Handel the Thunderbolt because he composed such an enormous amount of music.

Rock Group Nametags

The Beatles
This group named themselves after the popular American group the Crickets. (Beetles is the British term for crickets.) The group's drummer, Richard Starkey, renamed himself Ringo Starr, because he liked to wear lots of rings.

The B-52's
See "Some 'Hairy' Tales," above.

The Cars
This group wanted a name that was simple and fit their sound. Inspiration struck during a ride in one member's Volkswagen. Their engine stopped running in 1988 when they broke up.

Erasure
British composer-singer-multi-instrumentalist Vince Clark and lyric writer–singer Andy Bell took this name from one of the song titles in their 1988 hit album "Chains of Love."

Eurythmics
The word *eurythmics* comes from the Greek word for well-arranged proportion and harmony in design. That's exactly what this group aims for.

Indecent Obsession
This Australian trio got the idea for their name from a novel called *The Thornbirds*. It was about a girl with a lifelong romantic obsession.

Kodo
In Japanese, *kodo* means "children of the drum." This internationally popular band uses traditional Japanese drums, including one nine hundred-pound, four-foot-high model.

Thompson Twins
Neither of the two current members is named Thompson, but they are twins. The name came from two British comic-strip detectives called Thompson & Thompson.

UB40
This British reggae octet—that's eight group members—took its name from a British unemployment benefit form. Proof positive that catchy names are wherever you look!

Named for Their Faves

Not since the Beatles stirred up a fan fever of Beatlemania have there been so many neat names to give fans a name link to their favorite stars. One of our kid consultants suggested *Homeworkers* for fans of the group Homework. Can you add to the list below?

Blockheads

All these fans made the New Kids on the Block the biggest teen group sensation of 1989, 1990, 1991, and ???? The Kids are all boys, which perhaps explains why the blockheads are mostly girls.

Bon Jos

The Bon Jos love Jon Bon Jovi, and he considers them so important that he once invited fifty of them to help him pick the tune names for one of his albums ("Slippery When Wet"). That's fan power!

Hammerheads

The Hammerheads are fans who are hot for M. C. Hammer's rapping and dancing.

VIPs

This nickname is an acronym (made up from first letters) for the Vanilla Ice Posse, which first formed in 1990. That's when rapper Vanilla Ice hit the road with M. C. Hammer and moved from show opener to show stopper.

Initials Plus Cool, Quick Names Mean "Rappers at Work"

New groups may push today's stars out of the spotlight. But as long as rapping's what's happenin', rappers will move those initials and cool little words around to create new nametags. The initials *D J* usually stand for disc jockey. That's rap talk for someone who plays around with two record turntables and a piece of equipment called a mixing board to create a scratchy sound. The initials *M C* stand for master of ceremonies. For the name behind the M. C. who became a 1990 crossover superstar, check out the last section in this chapter, "Music Stars with Sports Connections."

Name: DJ Jazzy Jeff & The Fresh Prince, the first rap act to win a Grammy (in 1988).

Who's Rapping: Jeff Towns and Will Smith.

Name: J. J. Fad, a California female rap group formed in 1988.
Who's Rapping: M. C. J. B. (Juana Burns), Baby-D (Dania Birks), and Sassy C (Michelle Franklin).

Name: L. L. Cool J, the first rapper to make the charts, says his name stands for "Ladies love Cool James."
Who's Rapping: Todd Smith.

Name: Run-D.M.C., rappers from Queens, New York; a group formed in 1986.
Who's Rapping: Joseph Simmons (Run) and Darryll McDaniels (DMC), with DJ Jason Mizell, also known as Jam Master Jay.

Name: Salt-N-Pepa, three female rappers from Queens who made the popularity charts in 1987 with "Push It."
Who's Rapping: Cheryl "Salt" James and Sandy "Pepa" Denton, with DJ Spinderella.

Name: Soul II Soul, two songwriters-producers-arrangers whose slogan is "a happy face, a thumpin' bass, for a loving race." Their first album, "Keep On Movin'," sold a million copies and won a Grammy Award.
Who's Rapping: Jazzy B. and Nelson Hooper, plus a nonfixed lineup of singers and musicians.

Famous Alliterative Names

Can you think of any other singers or groups besides the ones below whose first and last names start with the same letters and sounds?

Adam Ant. English pop star and actor, born Stuart Goddard.
Bobby Brown. Rhythm and blues singer.
Carlene Carter. Third-generation country singer.
Duranduran. Band formed in Birmingham, England, in 1980. Originally spelled Duran Duran. (*This list continues on p. 36.*)

THEIR NAMES ARE ON THE MAP

Place	*Musician or Group*
TOWNS/CITIES	
Conway, Ark. and Twitty, Tex.	Country star Conway Twitty; born Harold Lloyd Jenkins.
Ladysmith Township, Natal Province, South Africa	Ladysmith Black Mambazo; vocal group with rhythms based on South African work songs.
Boston	Rock group from Boston; since the 1970s.
STATES	
Alabama	The three cousins who started the group of this name are all from Alabama.
Kentucky	Kentucky Headhunters; country rock group that moved into big time with 1990 Grammy and American Music awards.
COUNTRIES	
America	The group America started with three guitar players who met in London at the U.S. Air Force Base. They currently work as a twosome.
CONTINENTS	
Europe	The group called Europe is Swedish. They named themselves for a continent because they hoped to make a name for themselves in many countries. And they did!
Asia	The members of the supergroup Asia are all English.

Janet Jackson. The Jackson Five's baby sister, who became even more famous than her brother Michael.

Joan Jett. Rock guitarist. Her 1990 album truly lived up to its name. You guessed it—"The Hit List."

Kris Kristofferson. Long-time country music–rock favorite.

Libby Larsen. Contemporary classical music composer.

Lisa Lisa. The most visible member of the pop dance trio Lisa Lisa and Cult Jam.

Lyle Lovett. Country singer who with his Large Band won a 1989 Grammy Award.

Melissa Manchester. Singer-composer-pianist.

Mitch Miller. Television conductor who rearranged a Civil War marching song as "The Yellow Rose of Texas."

Ricki Rockell. Drummer with Poison.

Tico Torres. Drummer with Bon Jovi.

Travis Tritt. Country music singer.

Tatiana Troyanos. Opera singer.

Tina Turner. Long-time rock star.

Tommy Tune. Singer, dancer, choreographer, director, and the 1990 winner of the Jean Cocteau International Style Award for his innovative style and "presence" in the theater.

Musical "Royals"

THREE LADIES, A PRINCE, AND A DUKE

Prince Roger Nelson
This instrumentalist-composer-producer-actor was named for his father's band, the Prince Rogers Trio.

The First Lady of Country Music: Tammy Wynette
Tammy is known for her tearful sounding voice.

Lady Soul: Aretha Franklin
Aretha has had albums in the top forty for more than twenty years, many of them gold records.

Duke Ellington: Edward Kennedy Ellington
Duke Ellington was one of America's most outstanding jazz

pianists and composers. He also led a band that toured all over the world.

Lady Day: Billie Holiday
Lady Day's unique voice will always be remembered by jazz lovers.

KINGS OF THE MUSICAL KINGDOM

The King: Elvis Presley
The King was also known as *Elvis the Pelvis*, a nickname that described the way he jiggled and wiggled his body.

The King of Jazz: Paul Whiteman
The 1940s were known as the big band era. Paul Whiteman led one of the biggest of the big bands. He was also the musician who persuaded George Gershwin to write the most famous classical jazz composition of our time, "Rhapsody in Blue."

The King of Swing: Benny Goodman
Goodman was the clarinet-playing bandleader who made famous the jazz style known as swing.

King of the Cowboys: Roy Rogers
This singing cowboy was known to every movie fan during the 1940s. His horse Trigger was equally famous, even though it didn't sing.

King of the Twelve-String Guitar: Leadbelly
Huddie Ledbetter, who lived from 1885 to 1949, was an inspiration for many folk and blues musicians.

The March King: John Philip Sousa
This all-American composer and bandleader made march bands sound more like orchestras. His most famous march was, and still is, "The Stars and Stripes Forever."

The Waltz King: Johann Strauss
Strauss's beautiful waltzes, especially "The Blue Danube," brought fame to his native city of Vienna.

SONG QUEENS

Queen Latifah
Dana Owens is a self-crowned queen. In 1990, just before her twentieth birthday, her first album, "All Hail to the Queen," rose to the top of both the pop and rap charts.

Queen of Soul: Patti LaBelle
Patti LaBelle began her career as the leader of a quartet called the Blue Belles, then struck out on her own in 1975. Her very first solo record, "Lady Marmalade," was a no. 1 hit.

The Queen of Jazz: Ella Fitzgerald
The most honored jazz singer of all time was discovered during an amateur hour in Harlem, New York, in 1934.

The Queen of Country Music: Kitty Wells
Kitty was country music's first female star. Every record she cut made it to the country music charts.

The Queen of Radio: Jessica Dragonette
Dragonette reigned during the pre-television 1930s. Tens of millions of fans listened to her weekly radio program.

Musical "Mothers" and "Fathers"

The Father of Music: Guido D'Arezzo
This Greek priest who lived in the first century A.D. invented the four-line staff for written notes.

The Father of Musicians: Jubal
The Old Testament describes Jubal as being the "father of all such as handle the harp or organ." Musical innovators have been called fathers or mothers ever since.

The Father of Rock 'n Roll: Chuck Berry
Berry's songs "Maybelline," "Roll Over, Beethoven," and "Johnny B. Goode" have become rock classics.

Mama Africa: Miriam Makeba
Makeba was known as the voice of black Africans in exile from South Africa's former apartheid government.

The Father of Bluegrass: Bill Monroe
Monroe brought the fast-moving folk-music style of bluegrass for stringed instruments and the voice to the public's attention. He also created its name, after the nickname of his home state of Kentucky, the bluegrass state.

The Father of Western Swing: Bob Wills
This entertainer, who lived during the early part of this century, was probably one of our first crossover artists. His music cut across the boundaries of blues, jazz, country, sacred, and pop music.

The Father of the Blues: W. C. Handy
Handy's compositions "Memphis Blues" (published in 1912) and "St. Louis Blues" (1914) made the blues popular throughout the United States.

The Father of Ragtime: Scott Joplin
Ragtime is a style of piano playing with an up-and-down or "ragged time" rhythm. It probably originated with the African-American style of dancing called *Ragging*. With his composition "Maple Leaf Rag" Joplin made *Ragging* an international dance craze. Eventually, ragtime was replaced by jazz.

Ma Rainey: Gertrude Pridgett
Ma Rainey was the first of the great blues singers. In 1900, when she was just eighteen, she married a minstrel-show manager and became Ma to his Pa.

Daddy Rice: Thomas Dartmouth Rice

During the early part of the nineteenth century, Rice turned the shuffling motions of an old, crippled slave into the first black-face musical act.

The Father of Gospel Music: Tom Dorsey

Dorsey wrote more than one thousand songs, including "Precious Lord, Take My Hand."

The Father of Impressionistic Music: Claude Debussy

This French composer worked and lived at the same time as the French Impressionist painters like Auguste Renoir. In the same way that their paintings gave impressions of scenes instead of photographlike pictures, Debussy's music was more about feelings than actions.

 THE FAMILY CONNECTION

Everybody's heard the expression, "It runs in the family." This is certainly true in music. Many of our musical greats had at least one relative who set them an example or encouraged or taught them. The family ties among today's musicians are as strong as ever. Many children of musical stars continue in the family tradition, and the popularity charts are packed with family acts.

Six Musical Dynasties

The Amazin' Jacksons

The Jackson brothers and sisters (see Chapter 9, "Four Super Singing Groups") were taught by their musician father. They added an important chapter to the story of pop music and went from a successful family act to even more successful solo careers.

The Family that Jams Together: The Marsalis Clan

This is one family that has no generation gap when it comes to musical taste. When the Marsalis clan of New Orleans has

SUPERSTAR CHILDREN OF SUPERSTAR PARENTS

Famous Parent	Famous Children
Nat King Cole	Natalie Cole
Judy Garland	Liza Minnelli
Cissy Houston	Whitney Houston (also a cousin of Dionne Warwick)
John Lennon (The Beatles)	Julian Lennon
Rick Nelson	Gunnar and Matthew Nelson
John and Michelle Phillips (The Mamas and the Papas)	Chynna Phillips (Wilson Phillips)
Brian Wilson (The Beach Boys)	Carnie and Wendy Wilson (Wilson Phillips)
Hank Williams	Hank Williams, Jr.

a musical get-together, the sound of their music is sure to be jazz—from the piano rhythms of fifty-five-year-old head of the family Ellis Marsalis down to the drumbeats of fourteen-year-old Jason. Now that Wynton (trumpet) and Branford (saxophone) have become world-famous bandleaders, the family rarely plays together in public. Together and individually, they've done more than anyone else to spread interest in this style of music among young musicians.

The Carters of Country Music
The Carter family first recorded their unique sound in 1927. Since then there's never been a time without a Carter family act in country music. The currently active Carters include June, one of the original family's three daughters; her daughters Carlene and Rosey; June's husband (Johnny Cash), and her stepdaughter, Roseanne Cash.

The First Families of Folk Music: The Guthries and the Seegers
Ruth Crawford Seeger was an American composer who lived during the first half of this century. She was the first woman

to be awarded a Guggenheim Fellowship to study music. During the Great Depression of the 1930s she became a music teacher to help support her growing family. After she started to collect and write down folk songs for her students she came to regard preserving existing music as being more important than composing. Her children (including songwriter-singer Pete Seeger) have carried on her work. The Seegers' enthusiasm was shared by Woody Guthrie, one of the heroes of modern folk music and the author of a thousand songs (including "This Land Is Your Land"). His son Arlo also became a folksinger. Today Arlo's son heads a group called Xavier.

The Fiddling Fiedlers

At one time there were so many Fiedlers associated with the Boston Symphony that people assumed they were all related. The most famous Fiedler, Arthur, conducted the Boston Pops for fifty years. Other Fiedlers who've "fiddled" with the Boston Symphony orchestra in some way include his father, two uncles, and a cello-playing cousin.

A Hundred and Some Bachs

Since the year 1580, close to 100 musical Bachs have made their livings as musicians. Annual Bach get-togethers were a feast of music. Johann Sebastian, the brightest star in this galaxy, had four sons who each became successful musicians. Skid Row's lead singer, Sebastian Bach, is *not* a descendant of this famous clan.

 # MUSICALLY GIFTED KIDS

Ever since the rise of public concerts in the eighteenth century, child performers have been a regular part of the concert scene. A musical prodigy is not just an early starter but a very young kid who composes or performs at the genius level. True-blue prodigies aren't just flash-in-the-piano (or violin, etc.) virtuosi, but instead outlast the novelty of being talented and young.

Prodigies Who Made Musical History

You've already met in Chapter 1 a number of musical prodigies who composed and performed in public before their tenth birthdays. Here are some more musicians who grew from being musical whiz kids to mature musicians.

Lorin Maazel (Conductor, b. 1930)

The 1939 New York World's Fair was filled with wonders. One of these was nine-year-old Lorin Maazel. He conducted two major symphony orchestras before age thirteen and went on to a successful career as an adult conductor.

Milton Babbitt (Composer, b. 1916)

Milton Babbitt was both a musical and a math whiz kid. He could identify classical music recordings and mentally tally his mother's grocery bill when he was just two years old. At five, he made his violin debut and composed his first concerto. Like many teenagers, he loved dance music. Being a prodigy he didn't just dance, but also performed with and composed songs for several bands. Later, as an electronic music pioneer he worked with a giant synthesizer made by the RCA Corporation. It took up an entire wall and was extremely complicated, a far cry from the synthesizers we know today. As a teacher and the founder of the Electronic Music Center Babbitt influenced many other musicians.

Yehudi Menuhin (Violinist, b. 1916)

Menuhin made his violin debut wearing the short pants then fashionable for seven-year-old boys. His sisters were also talented, but like other sisters of musical brothers their talents took second place to Yehudi's. (Other examples: Nannerls Mozart and Fanny Mendelssohn.) Menuhin outgrew his short pants, but never his talent.

Louis Moreau Gottschalk (Composer-pianist, 1829–1869)

Gottschalk was America's first prodigy. He played the violin at six, the piano at twelve, and always performed his own compositions, even at his concert debut. He is also known for several postprodigy firsts. He was the first American idol (women fans used to rush onstage and fight over the white gloves he always wore on stage), the first American international star, and the first composer to introduce Latin-American rhythms into his compositions.

Stephen Collins Foster (Composer, 1826–1864)
America's best-loved songwriter played the flute at age four and completed his first composition at age fifteen. His songs captured the spirit and flavor of America and have remained popular throughout the years.

Jacques Offenbach (Composer, 1819–1880)
Offenbach was an excellent violin player at six, composed at eight, and played the cello at nine. The Tales of Hoffmann was his most famous work. And one of his least-known works became very important to the United States Marines. Check it out in Chapter 9.

Sergei Prokofiev (Pianist-composer, 1891–1953)
Prokofiev performed as a pianist at six and composed an opera at nine. His "Peter and the Wolf" is one of the best-selling gift albums for kids of all ages.

Today's Prodigies . . . Tomorrow's Legends

The following list of modern prodigies is especially notable for one fact. All those on it have led more normal childhoods than the prodigies of the past. Even though they spend many hours practicing, they also manage to go to school and enjoy other activities.

Jacob Armen
Jacob's father, a music teacher, sat him down at a drum set when he was just a year and a half old. He was only six when he made a sensational solo appearance at the Monterey Jazz Festival.

Joshua Bell
In 1981, fourteen-year-old Joshua Bell became the youngest violinist to appear as a soloist with the Philadelphia Orchestra. While still in his teens he was the subject of a movie. Joshua is very much an example of a prodigy who has always managed to have fun. He plays tennis, soccer, basketball, football, racquetball, and golf.

Christopher Gauthier
Cello prodigies are somewhat newer to the concert stage than violinists and pianists. Christopher Gauthier is one of them. He had chalked up three solo appearances with the Philadelphia Orchestra by the time he was thirteen years old.

Matt Haimovitz
This Israeli-born cellist was "discovered" by a violinist (Itzhak Perlman) when he was ten. He practiced four hours a day throughout his high school days but also found time for sports and friends.

Leila Josefowicz
Violinist Leila Josefowicz was only ten when she performed at the opening of the Bob Hope Cultural Center, but she had already had seven years of public concert experience. No wonder she didn't sneak even one nervous look at the President of the United States, who was in the audience. She attends public school and practices for three to four hours a day.

Evgeny Kissin
Moscow-born Evgeny began picking out melodies on the piano at age two. He attended a school for musically gifted children and made his debut at age ten. By the time he made his 1990 New York debut he was an "old man" of eighteen and already a recording star.

Midori (Mi Dori Goto)
This Japanese violin virtuoso was still playing a child's violin when she calmly went through the violinist's version of a trial

by fire—not one, but two strings broke during a concert. Instead of leaving the stage when her own string broke, she took the first violinist's full-sized instrument. When a string broke again, she switched instruments once more—all in the space of a second! Her musical history didn't begin with that broken string, but with her first lessons at age four. Her star as a concert artist continues to soar.

MUSICIANS WHO TRIUMPHED OVER HANDICAPS

_ho:

Stevie Wonder.
Multitalented rock and soul superstar since age thirteen.

_hat Happened:

Blind since birth and without his sense of smell since a 1973 auto accident, he's more accomplished than most people with all their five senses.

_ho:

Jeff Healey.

_hat Happened:

This Canadian blues-rock guitarist was blinded by cancer at age one. He plays with his instrument held flat in his lap and has been a superstar since 1989.

_ho:

Itzhak Perlman.

_hat Happened:

This superstar of the concert stage was stricken with polio as a child. But once he puts down his crutches and picks up his violin, people forget everything except his music. He is an active spokesperson for access to places of entertainment for the handicapped.

_ho:

Paul Wittgenstein.

_hat Happened:

Many pianists have lost the use of an arm, either through injury or overuse. Thanks to Wittgenstein, who lost his arm as a soldier, much music has been written especially for one-handed pianists.

Who:
Bret Michaels.
What Happened:
One of the hard-rock group Poison's early songs, "Cry Tough," was about believing in yourself. Bret Michaels, the group's lead singer, has been doing just that since he was told he had diabetes at age six. He accepts his illness but does not allow it to interfere with his music.

MUSIC AND OTHER PROFESSIONS

Musical People Famous for Nonmusical Accomplishments

For another list of famous hobby musicians look under "Famous Amateur Players" in Chapter 7.

Fiorello La Guardia
This mayor of New York City was an enthusiastic concertgoer and amateur conductor. The New York High School of Performing Arts is named in his honor.

Pope John Paul II
When this pope recorded an album of original folksongs in 1979 he was following in the footsteps of several other composing pontiffs.

Bill Cosby
In April 1990 this popular comedian turned his lifelong interest in jazz into a record, "Bill Cosby and Friends—Where You Lay Your Head." Like many current albums, it featured lots of guest artists.

NONMUSICAL JOBS ONCE HELD BY FAMOUS MUSICIANS

Names with a * indicate that this person is a living musician.

Job	*Musician*
College Professor	*Johnny Clegg, South African bandleader
Doctor	*Jeffrey Tate, British conductor
Fashion Model	*Whitney Houston, pop music singer
Head of State	Ignace Paderewski, who interrupted his career as a pianist to become Poland's head of state
Lawyer	*David Zippel, lyric writer for the Broadway musical "City of Angels."
	Peter Ilyich Tchaikovsky, Russian composer
Mortician (also Disc Jockey)	*John Conlee, pop singer
Naval Officer	Nikolai Rimsky-Korsakov, Russian composer
Painter and Poet	*Patti Smith, electric guitarist/songwriter
Politician	*Peter Garrett of Midnight Oil. He was once a candidate for the Australian Senate.
Professional Soldier (also studied medicine and art)	Fritz Kreisler, famous Austrian-born violinist
Real Estate Salesperson	*Shirley Verrett, opera singer
Speech and Drama Teacher	*Sheena Easton, Scottish-born pop star

Norio Ohga

The president of the Sony Corporation of Tokyo was a successful vocalist when he was persuaded to switch to a business career. To honor his musical past Sony executives arranged for him to conduct the Tokyo Philharmonic orchestra on his sixtieth birthday.

Noah Webster

The statue at Yale University in Noah Webster's honor shows him with one hand grasping his dictionary. The other might well have held a flute. Webster was an excellent and regular player long before he began work on his famous dictionary and other textbooks.

Mark Twain

This famous writer often pretended that he didn't like music. The fact is that he taught himself to play piano by ear, and his public readings often included piano recitals. He also encouraged his daughter to study music and was an enthusiastic concertgoer.

MUSICIANS AND THEIR HOBBIES

The Hobby	*The Hobbyist*
Cartoonist	Opera singer Enrico Caruso
Collecting	Award-winning songwriter John D. Loudermilk collects hurricanes. He rushes to hurricane areas and collects the air in Mason jars.
	Violinist Jascha Heifetz collects violins, including one made in 1750 out of glued-together matches.
	Pianist-showman Liberace collected at least forty-five grand pianos and many miniatures.
	Composer George Frederick Handel collected many fine paintings.
Cooking	Concert violinist Itzhak Perlman was a "cooking" guest in 1990 on "The Frugal Gourmet" TV show.
Drawing and Painting	Pop singer Tony Bennett

MUSICIANS AND THEIR HOBBIES

The Hobby	The Hobbyist
Firefighting	Conductor Arthur Fiedler. His local fire department gave him an old pumper truck for his seventy-fifth birthday.
Kite Flying	Brazil's greatest composer, Hector Villa-Lobos
Gourmet (lover of good food)	Opera composer Gioacchino Rossini

SPORTS FACTS WITH A MUSICAL TWIST

Music Stars with Sports Connections

Paula Abdul

Before Paula became a choreographer and pop star she was one of the cheerleaders for the Los Angeles Lakers.

M. C. Hammer

When he was still Stan Kirk Burrell this rap star worked as a batboy for his hometown Oakland, California, Athletics. The players called him the Little Hammer. They thought he resembled Hank Aaron, baseball's home-run leader, who was often called the Hammer. The name stuck!

Barbara Mandrell

This country singing star sponsors several sports charity events. Her support got her elected to the Tennessee Sports Hall of Fame.

Richard Sterbon

This bass singer of the group called Oak is part owner of three minor-league baseball teams: the Nashville Sounds, the Greensboro Hornets, and Salem Redbirds.

Conway Twitty
Twitty was all set to sign a contract to play with the Philadelphia Phillies when he was drafted. That ball team's loss became country music's gain.

Cole Porter
This songwriter of many Broadway show tunes also wrote a Yale football rally song called "Bulldog! Bulldog!"

Gene Autry
After years as a singing movie and radio cowboy, Gene Autry traded his saddle and microphone for a baseball team, the Los Angeles Angels.

Charles Ives
This composer used his experience as a Yale student in a composition called "A Yale–Princeton Football Game." If you get the record, listen to the bassoons pushing and grunting like guards, the trumpet as "running halfback," and the sound of the singing and cheering crowds.

SIX ATHLETIC MUSICIANS

Name	Sport
Terence Trent D'Arby, pop singer	Former member, U.S. Army boxing team.
Placido Domingo, opera singer	Baseball and soccer.
Julio Iglesias, pop singer	Played soccer professionally.
Elton John, pop singer	A soccer enthusiast, he once toured China with the Waterford, Ireland, Soccer Club.
Madonna, pop singer-dancer	Aerobics, swimming.
Charley Pride, country music singer	Baseball.
Bruce Springsteen, rock singer	Weight lifting, running.

THE LANGUAGE OF MUSIC

3

D o you know why Bobby McFerrin's 1988 hit tune "Don't Worry, Be Happy" is an a capella song? Or why we call someone who's in good health "fit as a fiddle"? After you read this chapter you'll understand these and the many other fascinating terms and expressions that make up the language of music.

EVERYDAY EXPRESSIONS WITH MUSICAL ORIGINS

Word or Phrase: Beats the band.
Meaning: Anything unusual.
Origin: At the beginning of this century every town had regular band concerts. Although the concerts featured other acts, few of these ever got more attention than the band.

Word or Phrase: Blow (or toot) your own horn.
Meaning: To praise yourself.
Origin: Horn instruments make loud, attention-getting sounds. To blow your own horn is to tell people about how well you can do something.

Word or Phrase: Buy for a song.
Meaning: To get something very cheaply.
Origin: Long ago, minstrel singers often sold their songs for the price of a meal or a night's lodgings.

Word or Phrase: Canary.
Meaning: A female singer; also slang for an informer who gives away secret information
Origin: Both of these kinds of human canaries got their nicknames from the singing canary bird discovered in the fifteenth century on the Canary Islands.

Word or Phrase: Change one's tune.
Meaning: Change one's attitude.
Origin: Minstrel singers often changed their songs to suit the occasion and the audience.

Word or Phrase: Face the music.
Meaning: Not run away from trouble.
Origin: Many singers get nervous before they go on stage. If they want to be singers, however, they have to get out there and face toward the orchestra and the audience.

Word or Phrase: Fiddle around.
Meaning: Waste time.
Origin: The Roman Emperor Nero was very musical. It's said that he sat "fiddling" even when fire threatened to destroy the city.

Word or Phrase: Fit as a fiddle.
Meaning: Healthy, in good shape.
Origin: Fiddlers are not any healthier than anyone else, so this expression probably became popular because it sounds nice, just as the instrument does.

Word or Phrase: Get into the swing.
Meaning: Develop a rhythm in some physical or mental activity.
Origin: This used to apply only to dancing.

Word or Phrase: Harp on.
Meaning: To repeat something over and over or to nag.
Origin: Some ancient harpists were known to play on a single string to show off their skill.

Word or Phrase: It's a hit!
Meaning: Anything that's a commercial success, from a new song to a new type of detergent.
Origin: Samuel Pepys, who wrote a famous diary about seventeenth-century London, invented the word *hit* to describe a successful musical event he once attended.

Word or Phrase: Know the score.
Meaning: Have all the essential information.
Origin: An orchestra conductor must know the entire score (all the instrument parts) for a musical work.

Word or Phrase: Music to my ears.
Meaning: A pleasure; good news.
Origin: People have used this to express pleasure for hundreds of years.

Word or Phrase: Pay the piper.
Meaning: To make good on an obligation.
Origin: Pipers were seventeenth-century street musicians. People who listened to their music usually gave them some money to show their appreciation. Modern street musicians usually put out a hat or other container for the same purpose.

Word or Phrase: Play musical chairs.
Meaning: Frequent job or policy changes, usually in competitive situations.
Origin: In the popular children's game of this name players move when the music plays and grab a chair when it stops.

Word or Phrase: Play by ear.
Meaning: To act without a formal plan.
Origin: In music, to play by ear is to play from memory, without using written music.

Word or Phrase: Play second fiddle.
Meaning: To be in the second-best position.
Origin: The first and most important violinist in an orchestra sits in the first violin section, closest to the conductor. That's not to say that the violinists in the second section don't play as well as those in the first—they simply play different parts. The first violinist is also referred to as the concertmaster.

Word or Phrase: Prima donna.
Meaning: Spoiled, demanding person.
Origin: This Italian term for a female opera star got its meaning from stories about some prima donnas' fiery tempers.

Word or Phrase: Sing for your supper.
Meaning: Pay for what you get. Another way of saying "there's no free lunch."
Origin: Like "buy for a song," this phrase originated with the minstrel singers who entertained for their suppers and often gave away their songs in exchange for a meal.

FROM A CAPELLA TO VIRTUOSO: A DICTIONARY OF MUSICAL TERMS

See also:
Chapter 1 for definitions of various music styles and international dances.
Chapter 7 for instrument descriptions, nicknames, and abbreviations.
Chapter 8 for definitions of musical notation terminology.

A capella. To sing without instruments. This style has come a long way from the chapel or church songs of the sixteenth century. Today it applies to jazzy tunes like Bobby McFerrin's "Don't Worry Be Happy." It also describes the music of the award-winning group Take 6. Their voices, plus electronically amplified finger snaps, hand claps, and other human sounds make them sound more like a band of sixteen than just six a capella singers.

Accompaniment. The vocal or instrumental backup for a melody.

Album. A collection of recorded songs. Best-selling or hit albums usually include at least one hit song (see "Hit Single").

Arrangement. A changed version of a musical composition. The arrangement might change the style in which the music is played or the instruments used to play it.

Billboard charts. See Charts.

Bubblegum music. Music that's supposed to appeal mostly to pre-teenagers.

Canned music. Recorded music.

Charts. The most important test of a recorded song or album's success is whether it "makes the charts." Various popular song charts are published, but to most people "the charts" means the weekly lists published by *Billboard* Magazine. The first *Billboard* chart was a single list published in 1913 as "Last Week's Ten Best Sellers Among the Popular Songs." Today there are weekly and year-end Top 10 charts for pop, rhythm and blues, country, and other musical categories. The weekly charts are also broken down into the Top 5, 15, 20, 25, 30, and 40, plus the Hot 100 and Hot 200.

Classic. Any long-lasting song or musical composition. There are rock classics, country music classics, and musical theater classics.

Comeback. Many songs and performers have very short-lived periods of popularity, but there's always the chance that they'll become popular again. One way this might happen for a song would be for it to be used in a new movie.

Concept album. An album that has one idea that ties it all together, as, for example, songs from one area of the world.

Concertizing. What musicians who spend most of their time giving live concerts do.

Cover record. When one musician records a popular song, others often record their own versions or covers. The more a song is covered, the more money the songwriter earns.

Crossover. This refers to music and musicians who are not locked into a single style category. An example might be a country singer who mixes pop and rock sounds and develops fans in several musical categories.

Curtain call. Audiences' applause is a signal to the leading performer to come out from behind the stage curtain or the back of the stage. If people continue to applaud, the performer continues to come back on stage. Sometimes there's an encore, which means "more" in French.

Debut. A performer's first public appearance or recording.

Elevator music. An unflattering term for recorded music, often rearranged to be played with more stringed instruments. It's played in stores, offices, and, of course, elevators, to make people calmer or more productive. Elevator music is also referred to by its trademarked name, Muzak.

Go gold. See "RIAA," under "Short and Snappy: Musical Acronyms and Abbreviations," below.

Hit single. An individual song that's popular enough to be listed on one or more of the charts that keep track of the best-selling songs and albums.

Improvisation. Players and singers often add their own touches to musical works. Improvisation is sometimes called instant composition.

Keyboard side. In a concert hall this is the side where the audience can see a pianist's fingers.

Label. The record company that actually distributes the records, as in "she records with the XYZ label."

Legends. Performers whose fame lasts for many years, like the Rolling Stones, even sometimes beyond their death, like Elvis Presley or Roy Orbison.

Live music. Music performed before an audience, not *canned* or recorded.

Lip syncing. Pretend singing to prerecorded songs. Kids often lip sync to a record for fun. Singer-dancers often lip sync to their own prerecorded songs, because it's difficult to sing and dance without sounding out of breath.

Platinum. See "RIAA," under "Short and Snappy: Musical Acronyms and Abbreviations," below.

Pop. All commercially successful popular music.

Pops. Concerts that mix music from musicals or the movies with tuneful classical works.

Premiere. The first performance of a show.

Refrain. The chorus or repeat part of a piece of music.

Remake. A newly recorded version of an old hit song.

Score. The conductor's written version of a piece of music. The score shows all the instruments' parts. The performers use copies of their individual parts.

Sheet music. Printed song music and lyrics.

Virtuoso. An outstanding musician. If there are several of these talented musicians, they are called virtuosi, not virtuosos.

 **INSIDER TALK**

Electronic Music Terms

Digital sound. *Digital* means that recorded sound is changed into a series of numbers, or digits. These numbers can then be stored in any way that makes it easy to get at them, such as on a compact disc.

Echo. An electrically created effect to repeat an instrument's tone.

Midi. See "Short and Snappy: Musical Acronyms and Abbreviations," below.

Mixer. A rock music box that ties together all the parts of a sound system. It lets you blend or increase sound and make other adjustments to the recording tracks.

Reverb. An electrically created effect to extend a note on an instrument.

Sampler. A musical computer that stores sounds instead of letters. It takes any sound you enter and converts it into bits of digital information that you can play back later.

Synthesizer. This device creates its own sounds, which can then be changed electronically. Some of these, like the Casio Sampler, can store as well as create sounds.

Tremolo. An electric effect to change an instrument's sound quickly.

Vibrato. Like a tremolo, but for an instrument's high and low sounds or pitches.

A Rock Crostic

Here's a word picture of all the styles that are part of rock 'n' roll music.

```
                   (R) A P
               P (O) P
               A (C) A P E L L A
         F O L (K) R O C K
           C O U (N) T R Y
             W O (R) L D   B E A T
           C R (O) S S O V E R
H E A V Y   M E T A (L)
           S O U (L)
```

Short and Snappy: Musical Acronyms and Abbreviations

Acronyms are abbreviations that combine the first letters of several words into one commonly used word.

ASCAP.   American Society of Composers, Authors and Publishers. An organization that licenses the performance rights to its members' music.

BM.   Beautiful music, usually tunes featured on the *Billboard* Top 40 charts.

BMI.   Broadcast Music Incorporated. A performing rights licensing organization like ASCAP.

CD.   Compact disc. The most advanced type of recording, with the sound recorded onto a plastic disc and picked up by a tiny, high-speed laser. The laser reads the recorded information, ignoring any dust or other imperfections in the surface of the disc.

C and W.   Country and western music.

DJ.   Disc jockey. A radio station employee who plays records and talks.

Grammy.   Award for the record industry's top achievers. The name was abbreviated from an early type of phonograph called the gramophone.

LP. Sound is picked up by a needle that revolves at 33⅓ rpm (revolutions or turns per minute) around a plastic disc with a grooved surface. Because the needle picks up everything, including dust that may have collected in the grooves, the LP is gradually being replaced by the CD.

MIDI. Musical Instrument Digital Interface. A system that connects computers and electronic instruments.

MOR. Middle of the road. A general term for music considered acceptable to the largest possible group of listeners. It can be in any style, as long as it isn't too difficult and doesn't offend anyone.

MTV. Music Television. Warner-Amex's twenty-four-hour cable TV network.

R&B. Rhythm and blues music.

RIAA. Record Industry Association of America. This organization certifies whether enough copies of a record have been sold to earn a gold (500,000 +) or platinum (1 million +) rating.

VJ. Same as a DJ, but for television.

Musicians' Slang

See Chapter 7 for musical instrument slang.

Burn. To play with passion.

Clam. Hit a wrong note.

Dues. Musicians who have worked hard and experienced hard knocks on the road to success are said to have paid their dues.

Gig. A job either for a band or an individual performer.

Groove. The rhythmic feel of a song.

Hook. The catchy, easy-to-remember element in a melody or lyric.

Jam session. Musicians' informal, unrehearsed playing sessions. To play at a jam session is "to jam."

Lick. Jazz term for a few strokes of a musical phrase.

Pipes. A singer's voice.

Riff. Improvised or unrehearsed solo.

Wail. To wail is similar to *burn*, but it applies to voice as well as instruments.

That's Rapping

Backspin. A disc jockey's method for maneuvering records on a turntable to repeat important beats or phrases.

B-Boy. A popular male rap music fan or performer.

Blaster. A portable tape player, usually turned on very loud.

Cut. The portion of a song to be played over and over again.

Def. Satisfactory, as "That's a def number."

Fresh. Original.

Hip-hop. Music that lends itself to rapping.

Joint. The best, as in "It's the joint."

MC. A rap performer.

Scratch. To move a record back and forth under the needle to create a scratchy effect.

Throw down. To challenge or dare someone with a rhyme.

FANCY TALK

The Greeks Had a Word For It

The Greeks were the most musical of all ancient people. It's no wonder they gave us many of our musical words.

English Word	Greek Origin
Chord	*Chorde,* for "string"
Cymbal	*Kymbalon*
Guitar	*Kithara*
Harmony	*Harmonia,* for "fitting together"
Melody	*Melodia,* for "choral singing"
Music	*Mousike*
Notes	*Neume,* for "sign"
Orchestra	*Orchestra;* in ancient Greece, the space in front of the stage used by the chorus
Organ	*Hydrolis,* for "water pipe"
Rhythm	*Rhythmos,* meaning "to flow"
Symphony	*Symphonia,* for "harmony"

What's the Difference?

Cadenza and glissando. Sometimes a band stops to give a singer or instrument player a chance to display his or her special skill. Such solos are called cadenzas. A glissando is another "show off" technique. It involves rapid gliding movements that are best suited to the harp or the piano.

Consonance and dissonance. When certain sound combinations are heard at the same time, some are consonant, or pleasing to the ear. Others sound harsh, or dissonant.

Concerto, sonata, and symphony. A concerto is a piece of music written for an orchestra and one instrument. A sonata is written for a solo instrument, like a piano, violin, or clarinet. A symphony is like a sonata, but it is for the entire orchestra.

Legato and staccato. Legato means that the music you're about to hear will have a smooth sound, without any noticeable interruptions between the notes. Staccato means the opposite. It has a disjointed quality.

Oratorio and opera. These are both musical stories. An oratorio is a musical drama for the church. An opera is a music drama for the theater. Opera comes from the Latin for work, meaning "worked over" beforehand.

What in the World Does It Mean?

Étude. An étude is a composition designed to help instrument players develop their technical skills. Some concerts include student exercises because some composers, like Chopin and Debussy, added melodies beautiful enough for public performances.

Fugue. A fugue consists of different parts of the same melody, each following the other in quick succession. At its simplest a fugue works like a round where the singers all sing the same song but at different times (for example, "Three Blind Mice," "Frère Jacques"). A famous fugue by composer Domenico Scarlatti was a case of "the cat made me do it." His cat liked to walk across the keyboard of his harpsichord. The composer then captured the sound of the cat's walk in a fugue that practically named itself: "The Cat's Fugue."

Impromptu music. In classical music, *impromptu* refers to music that is supposed to sound as though it had been improvised or unrehearsed. Notice the words "supposed to."

Opus. Some early composers were so busy composing that they didn't have time to think up catchy titles. Instead, they just numbered each piece of work. However, instead of saying work no. 2 or whatever, they used the Latin word *opus*, which means the same thing. Something marked opus 21 or op. 21 would therefore be a composer's twenty-first work. In the title Opus 21, Symphony no. 3 the second part simply tells you that this also happens to be this composer's third symphony.

Variation. Variation is a composer's way of presenting one musical theme in different ways. No matter what the variation (different style, different instruments, or whatever) it always has something in common with the theme—otherwise it wouldn't be a variation!

MUSICAL FACTS ABOUT THE U.S. PRESIDENTS AND THEIR FAMILIES

4

A number of United States presidents knew how to play a musical instrument. Few had much time to practice, though two actually played the piano at public events. Whether they were musical or not, most presidents have played an important role in encouraging the performing arts. This chapter is a rare collection of facts about the presidents' personal and public musical lives.

MUSICAL INTERESTS OF PRESIDENTS AND THEIR FAMILIES

Nine Presidents Who Played Instruments

President: Thomas Jefferson.
Instrument: Violin.
Additional Facts: Jefferson was an excellent violin player by the time he was fourteen, and he described music as his "favorite passion." He was also one of the first Americans to own a piano and collected many printed musical works.

President: John Quincy Adams.
Instrument: Flute.
Additional Facts: Although he didn't play very well, President Adams enjoyed music and made sure that all his children had music lessons.

President: John Tyler.
Instrument: Violin.
Additional Facts: The eighth president came from a musical family. As president he was too busy to play the violin, but he did listen to music to relax. After he retired, he went back to his violin and often played at family get-togethers.

President: Chester A. Arthur.
Instrument: Banjo.
Additional Facts: The banjo was one of the most popular instruments at this time. People who knew President Arthur said he played quite well, but little is known about what he played. It's a good possibility that he played duets with his son, who was known to be an excellent banjo player.

President: Warren G. Harding.
Instrument: Alto Horn, Cornet.
Additional Facts: Harding organized the Marion (Ohio) Citizens' Cornet Band and played with them at both the Democratic and Republican conventions. During his presidency he sometimes picked up an instrument and joined in on the Marine Band rehearsals.

President: Calvin Coolidge.
Instrument: Harmonica.
Additional Facts: Coolidge was a shy man. If he played during his White House days, he did so when nobody was listening.

President: Woodrow Wilson.
Instrument: Violin.
Additional Facts: This president learned to play as a boy and continued to do so casually for many years. He was also a fine

singer. People greatly admired his ability to hold the high note at the end of "The Star-Spangled Banner."

President: Harry Truman.
Instrument: Piano.
Additional Facts: Truman studied piano from the ages of eight to sixteen. During his presidency he had a radio by his bed and a piano near his desk. Truman was one of the few presidents who played in public. During a nationally televised tour of the White House in 1952, he played bits of Mozart on each of the two concert grand pianos in the East Room.

President: Richard M. Nixon.
Instrument: Piano (also studied violin).
Additional Facts: Nixon played simple, popular music for birthdays and at Christmas parties and when he was alone in his private quarters. Blues singer Pearl Bailey once persuaded him to play any tune of his choice to accompany her at a dinner for the nation's governors. He played "Home on the Range." Two unfulfilled ambitions listed in his autobiography are to direct a symphony orchestra and to play a cathedral organ. In a tape for the Nixon Library, he said that if he'd been born later he might have been a rapper (really!).

 Four Little-known Musical Facts about George Washington

- Stories about his ability to play the flute and the violin are not true.
- By his own public admission, he could sing no better than he could play an instrument. That's not to say he didn't like music. He was once quoted as saying, "Nothing is more agreeable, and ornamental, than good music."
- More songs were written in his honor than for any other president. One of these, the "President's March," became the song played for all the presidents.
- Many people wanted Washington to be named king instead of president. Maybe this is why both "God Save the King"

and "The President's March" were played at his inauguration.

To Each His Own: A Look at Presidential Musical Tastes

George Bush

In 1990 President Bush wrote an article in which he explained that he likes country music because "it is real people singing real stories that we can all understand." He named Reba McEntire as one of his favorite singers. He and his wife, Barbara, also love classical music and often listen to recordings by opera singers like Leontyne Price and Placido Domingo.

James Earl (Jimmy) Carter

President Carter, a classical music and jazz enthusiast, had the stereo in his White House office going eight to ten hours a day. The music of Debussy, Bach, and Wagner was heard most often. When the famous bop artist Dizzy Gillespie once played "Salt Peanuts" for him, the president repeated the exclamation "salt peanuts!" during the breaks. It was probably the first presidential hot chorus in history.

Grover Cleveland

President Cleveland was a great fan of Gilbert and Sullivan's operettas. He was also the only president ever to get married in the White House. Can you guess what the Marine Band played when his wedding guests had assembled in the East Room? That's right: "And He's Going to Marry Yum Yum," from "The Mikado."

Ulysses S. Grant

Grant's reputation as one of our most unmusical presidents is based on a remark he may or may not have actually made. It goes like this: "I know only two tunes: one is "Yankee Doodle," and the other isn't."

Lyndon B. Johnson
It should come as no surprise that this Texas president's favorite songs all had a western flavor. He especially loved "Don't Fence Me In," all the songs from the musical "Oklahoma," and, naturally, "The Yellow Rose of Texas."

Abraham Lincoln
Although Lincoln was not musically gifted, music sometimes moved him to tears. He loved sentimental ballads and was also our most opera-loving president ever. When he was criticized for going to the opera (nineteen times) while the country was at war, he said that this was his only diversion.

Franklin Delano Roosevelt
Can a president turn an old, unknown song into a hit? You bet! "Home, Home on the Range" was published in 1910, but it didn't become a hit until 1933. That's when President Franklin D. Roosevelt declared that it was his favorite song. He was also fond of songs about the sea and had a large collection of sheet music of nautical songs.

Harry S Truman
Truman loved classical music, from the early composers like Mozart to Gershwin's "Rhapsody in Blue." He wasn't too fond of opera, though, except when his daughter Margaret, who had studied to be an opera singer, was performing. And even though he was born in Missouri, the "Missouri Waltz" wasn't high on his hit list.

Musical First Ladies

Louisa Catherine Adams
Mrs. John Quincy Adams' harp playing is recorded in a painting of the First Lady plucking the strings.

Ellen Arthur
President Chester A. Arthur's wife had a fine contralto voice and belonged to a well-known glee club.

Mamie Eisenhower
President Dwight D. Eisenhower's wife played both the organ and the piano. She was self-taught and played by ear. Her music making was limited to family sing-alongs.

Betty Ford
First Lady Betty Ford studied dancing before she got married. Her teacher, the choreographer Martha Graham, received the Presidential Medal of Freedom during her husband's administration.

Florence Kling Harding
Only two First Ladies have been musical "pros," and President Warren G. Harding's wife was one of them. She studied at the Cincinnati Conservatory of Music and taught piano.

Caroline Scott Harrison
This First Lady, a former college music teacher, played many White House piano duets with her daughter, Mary McKee.

Lucy Webb Hayes
The wife of President Rutherford B. Hayes spent many evenings singing and playing the piano. Hymns were the top songs at the many musical get-togethers held in their family quarters.

Eleanor Roosevelt
The wife of Franklin Delano Roosevelt enjoyed country dances and had a number of dances named in her honor. These included The Eleanor Waltz, The Eleanor Glide, and The Eleanor Walk. She explained her belief in music as an important international language in these words: "People can get together and understand each other while making music in a way that would be impossible were they doing anything else."

Helen Taft
Because Mrs. Taft spent so much time in the Blue Room, which

held her piano, this became known as the Music Room during her husband's administration. She was also the founder and president of the Cincinnati Symphony.

Little-known Musical Information about White House Residents

- Amy Carter took violin lessons during her father's administration. When she practiced her mother, First Lady Rosalyn Carter, often accompanied her on the piano.
- Although President Ronald Reagan's son Ron was a professional dancer and his daughter Patty a country singer, his own performing talents did not include music. When he was a movie actor he was once cast as a piano player. He had to practice for two weeks on a dummy keyboard to prepare for the part.
- President Harry Truman's daughter Margaret had a brief career as a concert singer. Her father was her first music teacher. She switched from singing to writing and is now a well-known author of mystery novels.
- Another White House Margaret, Margaret Wilson, studied singing at the Peabody Conservatory. She was about Margaret Truman's age when her father, Woodrow Wilson, became president. She performed at several formal White House events.
- Charles Gates Dawes was the first and only vice-president who ever wrote a pop song. He served with President Calvin Coolidge. In 1958 his song "Melody in A Major" became a top hit as a remake called "It's All in the Game."
- President Andrew Jackson's daughter was the first person ever to buy a guitar made in Nashville, Tennessee. Look for it if you ever visit the Jackson museum, The Hermitage.
- When President William McKinley was shot by an assassin his last words were from his favorite song, "Nearer My God to Thee."
- During the six short months James Garfield was president, he often slipped upstairs to hear his seventeen-year-old son Hal, a talented pianist, play.

- One of the most musically gifted White House residents ever was President Millard Fillmore's daughter Mary Abigail. She was a talented amateur performer on the harp, piano, and guitar.
- The record for the longest practice schedule for a White House kid goes to George Washington's adopted grand-daughter Nellie Custis. She often clocked in at five hours a day on the piano. Her grandfather spent more money on her music lessons than on any other part of her education.

Three Presidents Who Didn't Want to Be Hailed, and Other Facts about "Hail to the Chief"

Here are three presidents who thought playing "Hail to the Chief" every time they arrived for some state ceremony was a terrible idea:

- Grover Cleveland just plain hated the song.
- William Howard Taft grew so tired of it that he banned it for the rest of his presidency (though Woodrow Wilson brought it back).
- Calvin Coolidge got rid of it again, because he disliked a lot of fuss. In fact, he told the Marine Band to avoid all patriotic tunes when foreign guests were present. He said it was too much of a nuisance to be saluting and standing at attention all the time.
- The song comes from an Irish tune.
- Its first use for an official occasion was at a Fourth of July celebration attended by President John Quincy Adams.
- For many years "Hail to the Chief" was just another song in the Marine Band repertory. Then, in 1845, First Lady Julia Gardiner Tyler asked the Marine Band to play it whenever the president made an appearance. It's been a big deal ever since.
- "Ruffles and Flourishes," the short drum rolls (ruffles) and a two-note bugle call (flourishes) was an extra musical wrinkle added to the "Hail to the Chief" introduction around 1895.

TEN PRESIDENTS WHOSE WHITE HOUSE YEARS WERE MUSICALLY MEMORABLE

1. President and Mrs. Ronald Reagan's nationally telecast "In Performance at the White House" programs were designed to bring together established American performers and new, young talent. The first program featured an eighteen-year-old violin virtuoso, Ida Levin, and her former teacher, pianist Rudolf Serkin. The sixty-year age gap melted away as teacher and former student played individually and together. Another young-meets-old concert featured country music veteran Merle Haggard and twenty-year-old champion fiddler Mark O'Connor.

2. The practice of televising White House musical entertainments for all the American people to enjoy originated with President Jimmy Carter and his wife Rosalyn. Several of their programs were dedicated to native American music.

3. President and Mrs. Lyndon Johnson introduced the pleasures of crossover music to the White House. They invited both western and classical musicians and proved that you can mix and enjoy both. In 1964 President Johnson pushed through and signed a bill setting up the National Council on the Arts.

4. John F. Kennedy supported musical progress in several ways. He increased public interest in leading arts organizations by inviting them to put on shows at the White House. He also introduced youth concerts by and for young people. He gave all military service bands, not just the Marine Band, a chance to play at White House events. And he created the Presidential Medal of Freedom to honor distinguished Americans in the arts and sciences. Composer Aaron Copland and opera soprano Leontyne Price were the first musical medalists.

5. Dwight D. Eisenhower's cultural exchange programs to send talented people in music and other fields abroad did much to strengthen world friendships. Musical organizations like the New York City Ballet and the Boston Symphony Orchestra spread good will throughout Europe and the Soviet

Union. As a result of the People-to-People Program to help American artists enter foreign competitions, twenty-three-year-old Van Cliburn became the first American to win the Soviet Union's International Tchaikovsky competition. To round out his musical programs President Eisenhower enacted the National Cultural Center Act. This later became the Kennedy Center for the Performing Arts, which annually honors outstanding artists. The first musicians to be honored were singer Marion Anderson, singer-dancer Fred Astaire, composer Richard Rodgers, pianist Arthur Rubinstein, and choreographer George Balanchine.

6. Franklin Delano Roosevelt created the Federal Music Project, which gave music jobs to many musicians during the Great Depression of the 1930s. This had the additional benefit of bringing music into homes, schools, churches, and concert halls.

7. Herbert Hoover's major musical contribution was to sign the bill that made "The Star-Spangled Banner" America's official national anthem. His wife was an active supporter of teaching kids to sing.

8. Theodore Roosevelt actively encouraged the preservation of all native American music. He fought to end legislation that punished Indians who talked or sang in their native language. To convince his cabinet to give the Indians the right to their music, he once invited a group of Cheyenne Indians to sing at a cabinet luncheon.

9. President and Mrs. Grover Cleveland were the first presidential couple to publicly support music organizations. Mrs. Cleveland personally helped one young violinist, Leonora Jackson, to study abroad. Jackson became the first American to win an important international award, the Mendelssohn Stipendium.

10. Chester Arthur's administration started the tradition of East Room concerts for special guests. This was a double first, because the invited guests were African-American musicians, the Jubilee Singers from Fisk University.

VITAL STATISTICS ABOUT "THE PRESIDENT'S OWN," THE MARINE BAND

- The Marine Band is our oldest continuing musical organization.
- It was established by an act of Congress signed by the second president, John Adams.
- The band has played for every president of the United States except George Washington.
- It has played at every presidential inauguration from Thomas Jefferson's time to the present. It was Jefferson who nicknamed the band "the President's Own."
- The Marine Band traveled with Abraham Lincoln when he delivered his famous Gettysburg Address. And its drums beat somberly during his funeral procession.
- At one time, Marine Band members had to perform many nonmusical duties. Today music making is their only job.
- John Philip Sousa almost didn't become the band's most famous leader. You see, when he was thirteen years old, he wanted to join a circus band. His father, who was in the Marine Band, got him a job as an apprentice musician instead. The elephants' and clowns' loss was the Marine Band's gain.
- The band has been coed for over twenty years, but men still outnumber women in it.
- The band averages six hundred performances each year. These include appearances by soloists, small stringed instrument groups, and full orchestra concerts.

MUSIC JOBS AND AWARDS

I f you'd like to be part of the music business, or know more about how it works, you've come to the right chapter. You'll discover that many singers, like Tommy Page and Vanilla Ice, got their start as opening acts for star performers. You'll also learn that there are backstage versions of superstars who are known as superproducers. Naturally, those who become stars want their chance to glitter at the various award shows. These televised events pop up on the tube at a rate of about one a month, so it's good to know when the ones you enjoy most will be telecast.

MUSIC JOBS

Music is a gigantic business with a large cast of characters. Besides the people you see and hear, there are many more who work behind the scenes.

The Four Most Popular Music Jobs

Composer

A composer is a writer who works with musical notes instead of words. Getting the notes down on paper is only part of the job, though. The composer also has to decide which instruments should play them, and how fast or slow or loud or low. Here are some examples.

Type of Composer	Type of Music
Classical	Music for symphony orchestras, operas, and chamber music groups.
Popular	Song and dance numbers for musicals, bands, and singers. Some composers write their own lyrics, but others work with collaborators.
Movie Score Composer	Background music that creates a mood for a story.
TV Composer	Same as a movie composer, but for television.
Jingle	Singing commercials.

Conductor

To stand in front of a band and beat time may look like the easiest job in the world, but there's a lot more to it than meets the eye. The modern conductor is like a general who must figure out how something should be played—and then get the musicians to do it. Here are four types of conductors.

Type of Conductor	Type of Band
Bandleader	School, marching, or dance band.
Concert Stage Conductor	Symphony or opera orchestra.
Theater Conductor	Musical play or revue orchestra.
Choral Group Conductor	A group of singers isn't really a band, but large choruses do have conductors.

Musicians—Important Players

Concertmaster. The violin player in an orchestra who sits closest to the conductor. The concertmaster sometimes substitutes for the conductor.

Lead instrument player. The most important guitar or bass player in a rock band.

Orchestra or band member. An instrumentalist who performs regularly with a musical organization.

Soloist. A member of an orchestra or a guest performer who plays the music intended to highlight one particular instrument.

Singer

Having a good voice is the key requirement for a successful singing career, but it's not the only one. A professional singer must also be able to communicate with the audience and to memorize words. Many singers make their first public appearances with school or church choruses. Here are five types of singers.

Backup singer. Someone who sings a chorus or harmony part in a song (usually as part of a group).

Choir member. Someone who sings with a large group and gets an occasional solo part.

Lead singer. The main singer with a band or group.

Opera singer. Opera singers need acting and foreign-language skills as well as well-trained voices.

Singer-songwriter. Many modern singers write their own material. (Check out "Answers to the Most Frequently Asked Questions about Songwriting" in Chapter 9 for more about how performers and freelance songwriters work together.)

 ## Tips for Kids Who Want to Start Their Own Group

- Be certain that your group gets along with each other, enjoys the same music, and can put in the necessary time.
- Find a place where you can rehearse. Even if your parents don't mind the noise, it's best to check it out with the neigh-

bors. You may have to limit rehearsals to the hours when they're at work.

- Don't wait to be discovered. Get out there and volunteer your services for school events and parties.
- Check your library for books about how to break into the music business.
- Look at some trade magazines like *Musician*. Maybe you can all chip in and share the cost of a subscription.
- Be patient. Success takes time, patience, perseverance— and practice, practice, practice!

Warm-ups for the Stars

Rock performers use up tons of energy. Besides doing their acts, they have to get into and out of their show clothes and travel from stage to stage. So one reason for having an opening act, especially during a tour, is to give the stars a chance to get ready for their own act and catch their breath. However, the opening act's most important reason for being is to warm up the audience for the big moment when the stars come out. As you can see from the list below, today's opening acts might be tomorrow's Big Bananas.

ABC for *Bell, Biv, Devoe*
The trio Bell Biv DeVoe started out with a six-guy teen group (New Edition). When they brought six new kids, called ABC, to their January 1991 concert they came full circle—from being part of a new teen group to forming their own trio in 1990 to creating and promoting another group. By the time you read this, ABC may be topping the charts.

Indecent Obsession for *Debbie Gibson*
This Australian group was doing okay in their own country. But when Debbie Gibson toured Australia and invited Indecent Obsession to open her show, they were off and away toward international stardom.

New Kids on the Block for *Tiffany*
If you'd mentioned the New Kids on the Block in 1984, most

people would have said "New Who?" For four years the group practiced their act before small audiences. It was only when pop singer Tiffany gave them a chance to be seen and heard as her opening act that they started their long roll as a superteen group. Their first fans were Tiffany fans, who opened their eyes, ears, and hearts to these five unknowns.

Sweet Sensation, Rick Wes, and Tommy Page for New Kids on the Block

Once the New Kids became stars, they got a chance to give a break to other unknowns. Three of their opening acts who also moved into the big time are Sweet Sensation (a girl group), and solo singers Rick Wes and Tommy Page. The New Kids not only gave these openers a break but in Tommy's case New Kid Jordan Knight helped him write a song ("I Will Be Your Everything") and then sang backup with New Kids Danny and Donny Wahlberg, to help make the recording a success.

Vanilla Ice for M. C. Hammer

Vanilla Ice had made his "To The Extreme" album, which was doing okay. Then the hottest rapper on the rap-and-dance beat, M. C. Hammer, gave Vanilla Ice a chance to open for him during Hammer's 1990 tour. That's when the Vanilla Ice album caused a major chart meltdown. In fact, toward the end of the year it popped the Hammer album "Please Hammer Don't Hurt 'Em" off the no. 1 position it had held for three months.

Some Important Behind-the-Scenes Jobs

A and R (Artists and Repertoire)

This record company VIP (very important person) finds new talent and makes sure that they have the right material.

Arranger

Good arrangers, also known as orchestrators, can make good musical scores great and give new life to old songs. What they actually do is to rewrite music to fit a specific instrument, voice, star, group, or show.

Copyist

The copyist breaks down a musical composition into individual players' parts, then writes a score for each instrument.

Manager

Different managers do different things. Here are some examples:

Talent Agents.　These people obtain bookings and fees for the performers they represent.

Personal managers.　These managers work for a particular group and handle their bookings, contracts, and public relations.

Concert hall managers.　Their job is to supervise all the activities and employees at a concert hall.

Record Producer

The producer coordinates everything and everyone involved in making a record. Some concentrate on only the business details, but many get involved in everything, including creative decisions. Some play such an important role in their performers' success that they become known as superproducers. Three of rock 'n' roll's most famous superproducers are

- Phil Spector, a teenager who worked with many famous groups during the 1960s. He also developed a recording technique that layered many instrument sounds on top of each other. It was known as the "wall of sound."
- Berry Gordy, who started Motown Records.
- Maurice Starr, who invents and manages music acts and also writes their songs. (Check out "Starr-born Teen Groups" in Chapter 9).

Sound Engineer

This technician operates an important piece of equipment known as the sound board. It controls and combines many different sound elements at a live show or during recording sessions.

Studio Setup Worker

The setup person gets everything in place before a recording session. This cuts down on the costs for recording studio rental fees.

More Jobs for People with Musical Skills

Cantor

A cantor is an employee in a Jewish congregation who sings at religious services and also teaches.

Choir Director

This person is a church employee who finds and directs singers, plans musical programs, and handles the choir's budget.

Instrument Artisans

Artisans are people who like to work with their hands. Instrumental artisans fall into three categories.

Instrument builders. These artisans love the feel as well as the sound of instruments and look for new ways to shape or build them.

Repairers. These are people who fix everything from broken strings and bows to clarinet keys and drum heads.

Restorers. These specialists can make an old instrument sound and look as it did when it was new.

Music Magazine Editor

Imagine meeting all the stars and getting paid for it. Editors at fan magazines like *SuperTeen* do just that. Jobs like this call for having a good sense for news, the ability to plan ahead, and to write and use a camera. Most editors start out as assistants.

Music Therapist

These health specialists use music and musical activities to treat mental and physical disabilities. A therapist might teach a blind child to play an instrument, or help the elderly enjoy singing and movement activities.

Teacher

Voice and instrument teachers work at home, or in private or public schools. Some have become quite famous.

Writer

Music writers review records, concerts, and musical theater events. They also write music histories and biographies.

MUSIC COMPETITIONS

Musical kids can compete for everything from parts in school musicals to scholarships and important awards. The World Federation of Music competitions in Geneva, Switzerland, recognize more than eighty competitive events for young virtuoso players. This means that young musicians—and their parents and teachers—must pick and choose carefully what to enter.

Tips for Kids Who Want to Compete for Special Honors and Awards

If the thought of performing before an audience makes you feel like a dish of soft Jell-o, this is only a case of stage fright. It happens to many musicians. The best cure is to get out there and concentrate on the music, not the audience. Here are four tips to get you going.

- Look for competitions close to home. Events sponsored by community groups are usually listed on community bulletin boards or in local newspapers. Such events allow friends and relatives to attend and don't involve travel expenses.
- Once you have entered a competition, make the most of it. When your performance is over, put it out of your mind and enjoy the other contestants' music.

- Don't overdo things. By all means practice, but don't put too much strain on your body. There's no point to winning now if you're going to hurt too much to play or sing later.
- Remember that competitions aren't the only road to success. Some kids enter lots of contests, but some don't enter any. Neither master cellist Yo Yo Ma nor the Russian piano prodigy Evgeny Kissin entered any competitions as teenagers.

1-6 AND THE WINNER IS... ALL ABOUT THE MAJOR MUSIC AWARDS

Eight Important Annual Award Ceremonies

Watch your newspaper television listings for the day of the month, and for new award programs.

Award: Academy Awards
Date of Award/History: March. The Academy Award Oscars are the movie industry's most important awards. They include awards for best background music and songs. The nominations for best songs usually include at least two or three rock songs.

Award: American Music Awards
Date: January. An annual television music event based on records compiled by *Cash Box*, the weekly entertainment trade magazine. The award categories include pop, rock, soul, and rhythm and blues, country, heavy metal, rap, and dance.

Award: Country Music Awards
Date: April. This annual show by the Academy of Country Music celebrated its twenty-fifth anniversary in 1990.

Award: Country Music Association Awards
Date: October. Another country music ceremony, this one by the Country Music Association, is held at the Grand Ole Opry, in Nashville.

Award: Grammy Awards
Date: February. Since 1958 the Grammys have been the record industry's most prestigious awards. The name is an abbreviation of the name of the first popular phonograph, the gramophone. This is the only award show at which you're likely to see in one place classical musicians, jazz stars, and rock idols.

Award: International Rock Awards
Date: June. Started in 1989, this show awards an Elvis trophy, named after rock 'n' roll legend Elvis Presley.

Award: MTV Awards
Date: August. MTVs have been awarded and telecast since 1984. This ceremony is the only exclusively rock 'n' roll award show, as well as the only one that's not broadcast live. The decisions about who gets which awards are made by people in the music and video business but also by the general public.

Award: Tony Awards
Date: June. This theater industry award is named in honor of Antoinette Perry. For the many shows performed away from the Broadway theater district there are also the off-Broadway Obie Awards.

Who Got What First

- The first Tony and Obie–winning musicals originated with the same author—sixteenth-century playwright William Shakespeare. The shows were "Kiss Me, Kate" (1949) and "The Boys from Syracuse" (1963).
- The first rock musicals to win Tonys were "Hair" (1968), "Jesus Christ Superstar" (1972), "Godspell" (1972), and "Pippin" (1973).
- The first Tony winner to feature soul music was "Dream-girls," in 1982.
- The first musical to win a Pulitzer was "Of Thee I Sing," in 1932.

- The first musical to win both a Tony *and* a Pulitzer was "South Pacific," in 1950.
- The first Grammy Awards had just twelve categories (there are currently seventy-seven), and none were rock 'n' roll. Pianist Van Cliburn, who won the first classical music Grammy, later established his own award, the Van Cliburn Award, for promising pianists.
- The first Grammy-winning album from a television series was "The Music from 'Peter Gunn,' " by Henry Mancini, in 1958.
- In 1984 Michael Jackson became the first performer to pick up eight Grammies in a single year. Good going! But when it comes to the most awards over the years, the winners are conductor Sir George Solti (26), pianist Vladimir Horowitz (23), Quincy Jones (19), and Stevie Wonder (17).
- In 1990 the People's Choice Awards created the first award category for favorite performers, chosen by twelve twenty-one-year-olds. The first winner was Paula Abdul.
- The first movie with a complete rock 'n' roll musical background was *Flashdance*, in 1983.
- The first and youngest winner of a special Oscar Award was Shirley Temple, age six, for *Bright Eyes*, in 1934. Older movie fans still watch reruns of this one to hear her sing "On the Good Ship Lollipop."
- The first winners of the Grammy Living Legend Award, established in 1989, were Liza Minnelli, Willie Nelson, Smokey Robinson, and Andrew Lloyd Webber.
- ASCAP, the American Society of Composers, Authors, and Publishers, has a Pied Piper Award for people who have most advanced the cause of music. The first Pied Piper was pianist-composer Duke Ellington, in 1968.

All about the Award of Awards: The Grammy

The National Academy of Recording Arts and Sciences' annual selection of seventy-plus Grammy winners is a front-page news event. Sales of the winning records soar by millions of copies. So you see that the Grammys are not only big news, but big business!

Grammy-Winning Records and Albums (1980—1989)

Winning any Grammy is a big deal, but the single-song record and the album of the year awards are the biggest deals of all. The date of the Grammys is always that of the year before the date of the award ceremonies. In other words, the February 20, 1991, ceremony was for the 1990 Grammys, those records recorded between October 1, 1989, and September 30, 1990.

Year	Record/Artist	Album/Artist
1980	"Sailing," Christopher Cross	"Christopher Cross," Christopher Cross
1981	"Bette Davis Eyes," Kim Carnes	"Double Fantasy," John Lennon, Yoko Ono
1982	"Rosanna," Toto	"Toto IV," Toto
1983	"Beat It," Michael Jackson	"Thriller," Michael Jackson
1984	"What's Love Got to Do with It," Tina Turner	"Can't Slow Down," Lionel Richie
1985	"We Are the World," USA for Africa	"No Jacket Required," Phil Collins
1986	"Higher Love," Steve Winwood	"Graceland," Paul Simon
1987	"Graceland," Paul Simon	"The Joshua Tree," U2
1988	"Don't Worry, Be Happy," Bobby McFerrin	"Faith," George Michaels
1989	"Wind Beneath My Wings," Bette Midler	"Nick of Time," Bonnie Raitt

Win . . . Win . . . Win . . . Win—the Four Most-Talked-about Grammy Awards of 1990

Record of the Year: "Another Day in Paradise," Phil Collins.
Album of the Year: "Back on the Block," Quincy Jones.
Song of the Year: "From a Distance," Julie Gold.
New Artist: Mariah Carey.

More 1990 Grammyists

Pop Vocal Performance
"Vision of Love," Mariah Carey.
"Oh, Pretty Woman" (from "A Black and White Night Live"),
  Roy Orbison.
"All My Life," Linda Ronstadt with Aaron Neville.

Rock Vocal and Instrumental Performances
"Black Velvet," Alannah Myles.
"Bad Love," Eric Clapton.
"Janie's Got a Gun," Aerosmith.
"DFW," the Vaughan Brothers.
"Time's Up," Living Colour.

Metal Performance
"Stone Cold Crazy," Metallica.

Rhythm-and-Blues Vocal Performance
"Compositions," Anita Baker.
"Here and Now," Luther Vandross.
"I'll Be Good to You," Ray Charles and Chaka Khan.

Best Rap Performance
"U Can't Touch This," M. C. Hammer.
"Back on the Block," Ice-T, Melle Mel, Big Daddy Kane, and
  Kool Moe Dee.

Best Country Performance
"Where Have You Been," Kathy Mattea. Also best country
  song.

"When I Call Your Name," Vince Gill.
"Pickin' on Nashville," Kentucky Headhunters.

Best Jazz Performance
"We Are in Love," Harry Connick, Jr.
"All That Jazz," Ella Fitzgerald.

Best Classical Music Performance
Shostakovich, Symphonies no. 1 and 7. Leonard Bernstein, conductor; with Chicago Symphony.
Shostakovich, Violin Concerto no. 1 in A Minor. And Glazunov, Violin Concerto in A Minor, Op. 82. Itzhak Perlman, violinist; Zubin Mehta, conductor; Israel Philharmonic.
"The Last Recording," Vladimir Horowitz, pianist.
"Carreras, Domingo, Pavarotti in Concert."

MUSIC HALLS OF FAME

The Country Music Hall of Fame (Nashville)

This hall of fame is located in Nashville and has its own museum. The first members inducted were the Carter Family (country singers since 1927), Jimmie Rodgers, and Hank Williams.

The Rock and Roll Hall of Fame

To qualify for membership here, performers and songwriters must have been active in recorded music for at least twenty-five years. At the sixth ceremony (in 1991) the musicians inducted included the Byrds, John Lee Hooker, the Impressions, Wilson Pickett, Jimmy Reed, and Ike and Tina Turner. A Rock and Roll Museum, which was supposed to have been built in Cleveland several years ago, is sometimes called the Phantom Temple of Rock. Maybe by the time you read this it will be closer to becoming a reality.

The Songwriter's Hall of Fame (Nashville)

The Nashville Songwriters Association International organized this memorial to honor country songwriters. Its members receive a bronze hand holding a quill pen. This award is called the Manny, an abbreviation for *manuscript*.

National Academy of Popular Music's Songwriter's Hall of Fame (New York)

This organization was established in 1969 to celebrate those who create popular music. By the time you read this, the Academy will have set up a museum of music memorabilia near Carnegie Hall in New York City.

A Hall of Fame with Kids in Mind

Music Alive, a monthly magazine for grade- and middle-school kids, has its own Hall of Fame. At least six issues a year honor a musician or group in a color photo and article, plus an audiocassette and sheet music for a popular song. Following is a list of the musicians honored during the 1990 school year.*

Award Winners	*When and Why*
Janet Jackson	February. Janet was selected for her innovative album "Rhythm Nation 1814."
Phil Collins	March. *Music Alive* honored Phil because he has helped many needy people with his music, donating songs to benefit concerts and writing lyrics that help spotlight their problems.
Paula Abdul	May. The Hall of Fame put the spotlight on Paula as she started her dance to superstardom.

* If your school doesn't get *Music Alive*, ask your teacher to write to them at P.O. Box 430, Port Chester, NY 10573.

Award Winners	*When and Why*
B-52's	October. *Music Alive* chose this quartet to show kids that success doesn't always happen overnight. The group recorded their first top-rated hits ("Love Shack" and "Roam") only in 1990, after some twenty years in the music business.
Young M. C., M. C. Hammer	November. This double Hall of Fame story paid tribute to the continued popularity of rap in general and these rappers in particular.
Mariah Carey	December. This award was made shortly after twenty-year-old Mariah burst onto the music scene with a first record that stayed in the top spot for four weeks.

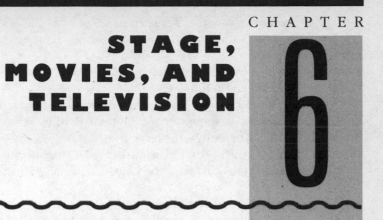

CHAPTER

STAGE, MOVIES, AND TELEVISION

6

Take a front-row seat for a look at the best musicals from the stage and movies. Amaze your friends with the fact that there's a musical that's been running for thirty years ("The 'Fantasticks") and that a rock star (Stewart Copeland of the Police) composed an opera. Discover the true facts about how the circus band keeps step with the horses and why the band plays only bits and pieces instead of whole songs.

MUSICALS
What Kind of Show is it?

Adaptation.   A musical version of a book or a nonmusical play, or a brand-new form of another musical.

Broadway musical.   The theaters on and around Broadway in New York City are where most big shows either succeed or fail.

Off-Broadway musical.   Some shows are best suited to small theaters away from the glittering lights of the bigger Broadway stages. Some start small to save money, then move to larger theaters later, when they have become successful.

Off-Off Broadway musical. These musicals are like the off-Broadway ones—but are in even smaller and less conveniently located theaters.

Extravaganza. A musical with very lavish sets and costumes, many performers, and a full orchestra.

Hot ticket. These are the musicals that are so popular that tickets, no matter how expensive, are "hot" or hard to get.

Movie musical. Currently, this term refers mostly to movie versions of successful Broadway musicals. During the 1940s and 1950s many musicals were produced especially for the movies.

Opera. A play with the words sung and few, if any, spoken parts.

Operetta. Operettas are like operas, but with less-serious stories and lighter music.

Revival. A new production of an old show. Some successful recent revivals of earlier hit musicals have included "Gypsy," "The Sound of Music," and "The Rothschilds."

Revue. Revues are made up of songs and dances, without any story.

Road show or touring company production. Successful musicals are usually performed by at least one company that travels to other cities and countries. Some continue long after the main show closes. That's why you don't necessarily have to come to New York to see a Broadway musical.

Giving Credit

Book by. The person who developed the dramatic plot for a musical.

Choreography by. The person who developed the dance routines.

Lyrics by. The person who wrote the words for the songs.

Music by. The person who composed the tunes.

Produced by. The person who put the show together—from raising the money to finding the theater to working with all the people involved in the show.

Great Musical Collaborators, Who Did What?

Irving Berlin and Cole Porter wrote both the music and the lyrics for their many hits. One of today's hit makers, Stephen Sondheim, also does both. But most musicals are collaborations. Some composer-lyricist teams last a lifetime, like Gilbert and Sullivan. Others change, for various reasons (Oscar Hammerstein collaborated with Lorenz Hart before teaming up with Richard Rodgers). As you read through the list below, see if you can think of a song from the shows mentioned. If you get stuck, turn the page upside down for a list of songs numbered to match each set of collaborators.

1. Andrew Lloyd Webber and Charles Hart. Webber and Hart are the team that produced "The Phantom of the Opera."
   Lyrics: Charles Hart.
   Music: Andrew Lloyd Webber.

2. Andrew Lloyd Webber and Tim Rice. Schoolmates who became a musical hit factory. Their shows include the rock musical "Jesus Christ Superstar" and "Evita."
   Lyrics: Tim Rice.
   Music: Andrew Lloyd Webber.

3. Martin Charnin and Charles Strouse. The team that produced the all-time kids' favorite "Annie."
   Lyrics: Martin Charnin.
   Music: Charles Strouse.

4. Rodgers and Hammerstein. This songwriting team's many hits began with "Oklahoma" and ended with "The Sound of Music."
   Lyrics: Oscar Hammerstein II.
   Music: Richard Rodgers.

5. Lerner and Loewe. Their most famous musical was "My Fair Lady."
   Lyrics: Alan Jay Lerner.
   Music: Frederick Loewe.

6. George and Ira Gershwin. "Oh, Kay!" was one of these supertalented brothers' first musicals. In 1989 it got a new lease on life with a new production featuring an all-black cast.
   Lyrics: Ira Gershwin.
   Music: George Gershwin.

7. Gilbert and Sullivan. Their operettas have a catchy, easy-to-identify style. "The Pirates of Penzance" first opened in New York in 1879. Over a hundred years later it returned to Broadway, complete with modern orchestration and a cast that starred Linda Ronstadt as Mabel.
   Lyrics: W. S. Gilbert.
   Music: Sir Arthur Sullivan.

Answers:

Top Songs from Shows by Top Composer-Lyricist Teams

1. "Think of Me" ("The Phantom of the Opera").
2. "Superstar" ("Jesus Christ Superstar"); "Don't Cry for Me, Argentina" ("Evita").
3. "Tomorrow" ("Annie").
4. "Oklahoma" ("Oklahoma"); "Climb Ev'ry Mountain" ("The Sound of Music").
5. "With a Little Bit of Luck" ("My Fair Lady").
6. "Someone to Watch Over Me" ("Oh, Kay!").
7. "I Am the Very Model of a Modern Major-General" ("The Pirates of Penzance").

Is It a Musical, an Opera . . . or a Popera?

Believe it or not, operas are as much about spectacular sets as are Broadway shows. Some productions of Giuseppe Verdi's *Aida*, for example, have live elephants on stage. They also have some pretty nontypical performances. Take, for example, "Holy Blood and Crescent Man," composed by Stewart Copeland of the Police, and Mozart's operas performed in modern dress and set in places like Los Angeles. At the same time, many Broadway musicals have operalike stories and music. Perhaps one day musicals like those listed below will be known as "poperas."

"Carmen Jones." This is a modern-day adaptation of the most popular of all operas, *Carmen*. It featured an all-black cast and was made into a movie.

"Les Miserables." This musical, often referred to as "Les Miz," successfully combines pop music with opera. It's based on a novel the composer Puccini tried to turn into an opera way back in 1862. He quit when he found the plot too complicated. Happily, Claude-Michel Schoenberg had better luck.

"The Phantom of the Opera." Who says a show with the "O" word right in a musical's title and an operalike musical score can't become a Broadway hit? Andrew Lloyd Webber's supersuccess certainly says it can. Did you know that it features some music from a couple of real operas, including one by the famous opera composer Giuseppe Verdi?

"Porgy and Bess." This American folk opera by George and Ira Gershwin was the first Broadway-to-opera-house crossover. People all over the world have seen road shows, revivals, and movie versions of it. The opera houses that have put it into their regular program schedule include the New York Metropolitan Opera Company.

"Sweeney Todd." Many traditional operas are filled with

screaming and tragedy. However, few are more grizzly than Stephen Sondheim's tale of a murderous London barber. It's been performed regularly in opera houses and on Broadway.

"The Threepenny Opera." Mack the Knife has been entertaining audiences for more than two hundred years. The original version, which was called "The Beggar's Opera," is known as the first musical comedy ever. In the most recent revival, in 1989, rock star Sting played Mack.

"West Side Story." Classical composer Leonard Bernstein, with lyricist Stephen Sondheim and playwright Arthur Laurents, created this exciting modern-day *Romeo and Juliet*. The show was like an opera, but with an up-to-date plot and tunes.

Four History-making, Record-breaking Musicals

"Jerome Robbins's Broadway."

When "Broadway" opened in 1989, audiences got to see a collection of the best scenes from choreographer Jerome Robbins' eleven top hits ("Peter Pan," "Gypsy," "West Side Story," and others). This musical of musicals featured sixty-two singers and dancers.

"A Chorus Line"

More than 6 million people saw "A Chorus Line" during its fifteen-year Broadway run. Millions more saw the touring company production. The show's simple story, an audition for a new musical, changed people's ideas about what a musical should be.

"Oklahoma"

"Oklahoma" won a Pulitzer Prize and was the first musical to have songs that grew out of its story. In addition to its 2,243 Broadway performances, the show toured over 250 cities over ten years. It also had road companies throughout the world and was the first complete musical ever to be recorded.

"The Fantasticks"

This off-Broadway show has run longer than any other musical in this century. In 1990 it celebrated its thirtieth birthday. Its road company has traveled to four major cities, three thousand towns, and sixty-eight foreign countries.

MUSIC AT THE CIRCUS
Six Facts about Circus Music

- Circus musicians are a busy bunch. They play throughout every circus performance. However, circus music is always in the background—and so are the musicians. This is not a job for players who want to be superstars!
- Songs are never played all the way through. After eight to sixteen bars, it's on to the next piece. A single performance might feature bits and pieces from as many as 120 pieces of music.
- Most music played during a performance is familiar enough for people to recognize without remembering the lyrics. The idea behind this and the constant tune switching is to avoid distracting attention from the performers.
- The circus has no one favorite musical style. Circus songs range from Broadway show tunes to fusion jazz and classical music.
- The busiest instruments at most circuses are in the percussion and brass sections. In recent years many synthesizers and electric guitars have found their way under the Big Top.
- If you've ever wondered how the animals learn to follow the music, the answer is they don't! The musicians keep time with what the animals do, not the other way around. Again, it's a case of the musicians following the stars, instead of the other way around!

Six Circus Favorites that Weren't Written for the Circus

Few composers are interested in creating music to be used mainly as background music. That's why the following popular pieces with circus themes and rhythms were not written specifically for the circus. Composer Igor Stravinsky did bring his polka to the Ringling Brothers Circus, but only after the Metropolitan Opera had turned it down. All the items on this list are popular ones in the circus band's repertoire.

Title	Composer
"Be a Clown"	Cole Porter
"Circus Polka"	Igor Stravinsky
"Entry of the Gladiators"	Julius Fucick, classical composer
"Follow the Band"	Cy Coleman
"Magic Razzle-Dazzle"	Kander and Ebb
"Men on the Flying Trapeze"	Anonymous
"Prancing Ponies" (circus name for "Fugue for Tinhorn")	Frank Loesser

MUSIC GOES TO THE MOVIES

A Screenful of Movie Firsts and Facts

- In the early movie days, music wasn't part of the movie itself. Instead, a pianist played the movie's music while it was being shown.
- The Tales of Beatrix Potter was the first original full-length movie ballet. Sir Frederick Ashton wrote the music and danced the part of Mrs. Tiggle Wiggle, the hedgehog.
- "Sonny Boy" was the first-ever movie hit song. It was sung by Al Jolson and sold over 2 million records, plus a million sheet-music copies.
- The most successful film composer of all time is John T. Williams. He wrote the music for *E.T. The Extraterrestrial,*

Star Wars, The Empire Strikes Back, Jaws, Raiders of the Lost Ark, Indiana Jones and the Temple of Doom, Indiana Jones and the Last Crusade, Superman, and *Born on the Fourth of July*.

- "White Christmas" was written for a 1942 movie called *Holiday Inn*. It was sung by Bing Crosby, whose recording of the song still outsells all other versions.

SIX MUSICIANS WHO BECAME MOVIE BIOGRAPHIES

Musician	*Movie*
Jim Morrison	*The Doors*
Buddy Holly	*The Buddy Holly Story*
Quincy Jones	*Listen Up*
Richie Valens	*La Bamba*
Loretta Lynn	*Coalminer's Daughter*
Wolfgang Amadeus Mozart	*Amadeus*

Six Movie Song Faves

All except one of these was a Broadway musical before it became a movie. Try to guess which one, before turning the page upside down.

Title	*Movie*
"Under the Sea"	"The Little Mermaid"
"Tomorrow"	"Annie"
"I'm Flying"	"Peter Pan"
"Aquarius"	"Hair"
"Boy for Sale"	"Oliver"
"Do-Re-Mi"	"The Sound of Music"

"*The Little Mermaid*"

Seven Facts for Wizard Watchers

- *The Wizard of Oz* was made into a musical by its author, L. Frank Baum, in 1903.
- The 1903 show was so successful that a takeoff on the story line, "Babes in Toyland," opened the same year. The music for it was composed by Victor Herbert, and it too was a hit.
- The original show and the megahit movie version had completely different songs.
- Dorothy's award-winning song "Over the Rainbow" almost got cut from the movie. Some people thought it was too slow.
- With the arrival of "The Wiz" on Broadway, in 1975, Emerald City became integrated (the cast was all black). It was also updated with a rock score.
- When British rock star Elton John sang "Goodbye Yellow Brick Road," he traveled all the way to the no. 2 spot on the charts. And he stayed there for fourteen weeks!
- The land of Oz that Rick Springfield had in mind when he produced his album called "Living in Oz" was the country of his birth, Australia. It's nicknamed Oz.

Five Walt Disney Movie Trivia Questions

What song from what Disney movie won a Grammy in 1990?
"Under the Sea," from *The Little Mermaid*.

What's the name of the dwarfs' marching song in Snow White and the Seven Dwarfs?
"Heigh Ho, Heigh Ho!"

What character in what movie sang "Hi-Diddle-Dee-Dee (An actor's life for me")?
Pinocchio, in the movie that has his name. This was Walt Disney's second full-length cartoon feature and the first to win an Oscar for its musical score.

What does Jiminy Cricket tell Pinocchio to do if he needs him?
"Give a Little Whistle."

Which Disney movie was made with a lot of classical music?
Fantasia. It featured the following music:

Title	Composer
Toccata and Fugue in D Minor	Johann Sebastian Bach
"The Nutcracker"	Peter Ilyich Tchaikovsky
"The Sorcerer's Apprentice"	Paul Dukas
"The Rite of Spring"	Igor Stravinsky
Pastoral Symphony	Ludwig van Beethoven
"Dance of the Hours"	Amilcare Ponchielli
"Night on Bald Mountain"	Modest Mussorgsky
"Ave Maria"	Franz Schubert

A VIDEO GUIDE TO MUSIC

See Chapter 1 for a list of MTV's top music videos for 1990.

The good news about musicals and movies and musical events available on video is that the list keeps getting bigger and better all the time. Anything current, like a hot new video by your favorite group, is likely to become available in all video stores. The bad news is that not every video store has the room to carry the thousands of videos available. For some of the older titles your best bet is to find a store that sells videos and nothing else, like the supermarket-sized Blockbuster stores that have sprung up all over the country. Many of the old-time favorites might also be available at the library.

★ Ten Videos by or about Rock Legends

"Dick Clark Presents 'American Bandstand' "

This video was made when this popular teen dance program celebrated its thirty-third anniversary. It's fun to compare it with what's on "Club MTV".

"Elvis— '68 Comeback Special"
There are lots of videos about the king of rock 'n' roll. This one shows him complete with sideburns and black leather outfit, doing lots of shake-rattle-and-roll songs.

"Girl Groups: The Story of a Sound"
All the big girl groups of the early days of rock are here: the Supremes, the Ronettes, the Shirelles, the Shangri-Las, and Martha and the Vandellas.

"Rock and Roll: The Early Days"
This video is a tell-all "rockumentary" about the good and the bad in early rock 'n' roll, with Elvis Presley, Chuck Berry, Buddy Holly, and Little Richard.

"Roy Orbison & Friends: A Black and White Night"
This tape features "Oh Pretty Woman" and other songs by this rock star who's become something of a legend since his death in 1988. Jackson Browne and Bruce Springsteen are two of the Friends.

"The Ladies Sing the Blues"
Here are sixteen songs by the legends of the bluesy rhythms so influential in rock: from the great Bessie Smith to living legend Peggy Lee.

"The Compleat Beatles"
If you want to learn what this fabulous supergroup looked and sounded like, this is the "rockumentary" for you.

"Tina Turner—Queen of Rock 'n' Roll"
What makes Tina Turner such an enduring star? Listen to her singing her biggest hits and find out.

"U2—Under A Blood Red Sky"
These twelve songs by this group of Irish rockers show why they became a superband, in 1988.

"Women in Rock"
Enjoy the sounds of the female chart toppers, from the early rockers like Carole King to Madonna, on this tape.

Historic Happenings

Concert for Bangladesh
Take a trip back to the first big rock charity concert. George Harrison, Bob Dylan, Ringo Starr, Ravi Shankar, and Eric Clapton are just some of the stars you'll see and hear.

Nelson Mandela's Seventieth Birthday Trip
This historic concert had an all-star cast. Songs you'll hear include "Brothers in Arms," by Dire Straits and Eric Clapton and "Amazing Grace," sung by opera star Jessye Norman.

The Wall
Several videos were made of the musical celebration that followed the 1989 breaking down of the wall that separated East and West Berlin for so many years. Look for the version that features Cindy Lauper and Sincad O'Connor.

We Are the World—The Video Event (1985)
Here's another superstar benefit concert. Maybe it will give you some ideas for things you and your friends can do to help needy people.

Movies about Kids

Amahl and The Night Visitors
Amahl, a young boy, is the hero of this first opera ever written for television. If you don't see it in the video stacks you'll probably be able to catch a rerun at Christmastime. You might even be able to attend a live presentation, for it's the most frequently performed opera in the United States and throughout the world.

Annie
This film brought a popular comic strip to life. Kids of all ages have loved the adventures of the little orphan girl, Annie, and her dog Sandy.

Bye Bye Birdie
This story, about Birdie, an Elvis Presley-like singer, was one of the first rock 'n' roll musicals to hit Broadway. Today's kids get lots of laughs from the old-fashioned clothes. They also enjoy rocking along to tunes like "A Lot of Livin' to Do."

Fame
This movie about life at New York City's High School of Performing Arts was such a hit that it became a television series. The music is flashy and fast moving.

Grease
There are rock musicals and then there's *Grease,* the pre-rock musical. The film stars John Travolta and Olivia Newton-John. Make sure you take out *Grease*, not *Grease 2*, which isn't as good.

Oliver
The movie is every bit as good as the original Broadway show. It's based on Charles Dickens's novel *Oliver Twist*, about a boy trapped into a life with a gang of thieves.

Peter Pan
Don't settle for anything less than the version with the original show's star, Mary Martin.

The Sound of Music
This story of a real family's escape from the Nazis during World War II won five Oscar Awards. Touring companies still perform the live version.

West Side Story
See and hear for yourself why this won ten Oscar Awards. If you've never heard the songs "Tonight," "I Feel Pretty," and "America," you're in for a treat.

The Wizard of Oz
Dorothy's adventures on the Yellow Brick Road, plus the many memorable songs, all add up to the hit of hits. Some kids have watched this ten times!

★ Nine Top Broadway-to-Hollywood Flicks

A Chorus Line—The Movie
This is the next-best thing to actually seeing "A Chorus Line," the live show that played on Broadway for an awesome fifteen years.

Damn Yankees
Good music and baseball—who could ask for anything more! The story is about a baseball fan who sells his soul to the devil to give his team a chance to beat the Yankees. It's a fun dance-along experience. Watch for the show-stopping "Whatever Lola Wants."

Fiddler on the Roof
The songs from this prize-winning musical have become wedding celebration standards. Listen for the gorgeous violin solos played by concert artist Isaac Stern.

The Music Man
This is a little old-fashioned, but worth watching, if only to keep in step with the "76 Trombones" march.

My Fair Lady
Here's another musical in the grand tradition that's held up well over the years. The songs most popular with kids are "The Rain in Spain" and "With a Little Bit of Luck."

The King and I
Great songs and beautiful costumes! This is the story of a governess in the household of the King of Siam and isn't the least bit dated.

Oklahoma
This is another old-timer with timeless tunes. The top numbers are "Oh, What a Beautiful Morning" and "Oklahoma!"

Pippin
In 1973 this won five Tony Awards. It's still a winner. Listen for the show-stopping "No Time at All."

Pirates of Penzance
This is an all-time Gilbert and Sullivan favorite. Stick to the version that stars Linda Ronstadt.

A Mix of Sights and Sounds

"From Mao to Mozart: Isaac Stern in China"
This documentary is about the world-renowned violinist's 1980 tour to China. It's a sightseeing as well as a musical treat.

"Making Michael Jackson's 'Thriller' "
Want to know how rock videos are made? This begins with the best-selling "Thriller" video, then shows how it was done.

"Paul Simon's 'Graceland' "
This is the video version of the 1986 Grammy-winning album

that led to the development of *world beat* as a musical category. Did you know that it was named after Elvis Presley's
mansion?

That's Dancing

Flashdance
Here's the movie that produced the no. 1 hit "Flashdance"
for Irene Cara.

The Nutcracker
This Christmas special is enjoyable at any time. Several good
versions are available. The very best one stars Mikhail Bar-
yshnikov with the American Ballet Theater.

The Red Shoes
The story's sad, but the music and dancing are wonderful!

That's Dancing
This is a movie anthology of dance scenes from popular movie
musicals. Super dancers and super dancing!

A "Read the Book, Then See the Video" List

Book/Movie	Author
Chitty Chitty Bang Bang	Ian Fleming
Doctor Doolittle	Hugh Lofting
Hans Brinker	Mary Mapes Dodge
Mary Poppins	P. L. Travers
Oliver Twist (Oliver)	Charles Dickens
The Wizard of Oz	L. Frank Baum

Videos for Fun with Kid Sisters and Brothers

"Charley Brown and the Peanuts Gang"
The gang made several videos. If you want to rest your eyes,
listen to the Charley Brown Anniversary cassette instead.

"The Great Muppet Caper"
If you've seen this before, you can always enjoy Joe Raposo's melodic songs, especially the Oscar-nominated "The First Time It Happens." If you can't find this, look for a series called "Sing-Along with Jim Henson."

"The Little Mermaid"
Don't take out anything except the 1989 Walt Disney movie. There's also a very nice listening version. (If you can't find it, call Dove Books at 1-800-345-9945.)

"Raffi with the Rise and Shine Band"
Two- and three-year-olds go wild over this Canadian folk-singer. He's made other videos, but this is one of his most popular ones.

"The Smurfs and the Magic Flute"
Oily McCreep steals a magic flute to get hold of an ancient kingdom's wealth—until the Smurfs intervene. Send mom and dad out of the room during this one.

MUSICAL INSTRUMENTS

CHAPTER

7

Having even a single instrument, like a guitar accompanying a singer, makes a tune more interesting. Combine that guitar with a harmonica and you've got the makings of a one-person blues band. This chapter is your guide to instruments used alone, by rock groups, and in symphony orchestras. One of the more unusual instruments you'll read about is a violin made from a shoe. There's all this, plus tips for selecting and learning to play your own instrument.

HIGHLIGHTS IN THE HISTORY OF MUSICAL INSTRUMENTS

From Old Bones to Million-dollar Violins

- The earliest musical instruments ever found are some 35,000-year-old mastodon bones from the ice ages. These musical treasures included two flute shapes, a beater, and several bone pieces marked to show their best-sounding spots.

- Ancient instrument makers used whatever was handy. Sometimes they even put live insects inside pipes to add sound effects. You might say that these buzzing bugs were the first back-up groups in history.
- Many early instruments were shaped to resemble animals. Some of these were named for their shapes, like the serpent that was a brass cornet, made from two pieces of wood bent and bound together.
- During the seventeenth century, a group of Italian instrument makers changed the violin's quality from good to outstanding. The best known of these artisans was named Antonio Stradivari. Most modern violinists would trade a brand-new violin for a real "Strad" faster than you can tighten a string. But ownership doesn't come cheap. A 270-year-old model once owned by composer Felix Mendelssohn recently sold for $1.7 million.
- Early electric guitars, especially those played by famous guitarists like Jimmy Hendrix, also fetch big prices.

Gods, Mathematicians, Bandleaders . . . It Takes All Kinds to Invent an Instrument

An Italian instrument maker named Mario Macferri recently perfected a plastic violin with top-quality sound. Another inventor, who practices law by day and works as a rock musician at night, developed a nonwarping guitar. Both of these men are following the never-ending trail of musical innovation.

Invention: Pan pipes (about 330 B.C.).
Inventor: Pan, an ancient Greek god.
Origin: According to myth (a type of Greek folk story), Pan reached out to hug a beautiful goddess. And she ran away he caught hold of a clump of reeds instead. His disappointed sigh ran through the reeds and produced a sad but comforting sound. To reproduce this sound, Pan broke off a bunch of the reeds and bound them up in unequal lengths. Believe it

or not, this small, simple instrument is the parent of the giant pipe organ.

Invention: Monochord (about 550 B.C.).
Inventor: Pythagoras, a Greek mathematician who with a group of associates first established a scientific basis for the study of acoustics.
Origin: Pythagoras' invention was designed as a tool to help change musical sounds by changing the length of a stretched string.

Invention: Glass harmonica, also known as 'Armonica (in 1763).
Inventor: Benjamin Franklin.
Origin: The glass harmonica originated with a system for making music by stroking the edges of glasses filled with different quantities of water. Franklin substituted different-sized bowls for the glasses. His bowls turned on a rod that was operated with a foot pedal. Several composers wrote music especially for this instrument.

Invention: Flute (in biblical times).
Inventor: Jubal.
Origin: The first musician mentioned in the Old Testament apparently wasn't content just to sing and play the harp. He also invented a flute and a small three-cornered harp called a *kinnor*.

Invention: Piano (in 1700).
Inventor: Bartolommeo Cristofori.
Origin: The first stringed keyboard instrument, the clavichord, was developed during the twelfth century. Its strings and keyboards ran alongside an oblong wooden box. Bartolomeo Cristofori improved on this with a system that used tiny hammers to strike the strings. People weren't very enthusiastic about his piano. However, this changed when two talented child performers, Wolfgang Amadeus Mozart and his sister Nannerl, caused a sensation when they performed on it.

Invention: Saxophone (about 1840).

Inventor: Adolphe Sax.

Origin: Sax grew up in his father's instrument shop in Belgium. With his father's help he developed a valved brass wind instrument with a new tonal quality, which he named the sax-horn (you can figure out for yourself how he came up with this name). Then he took his sax-horn to Paris, where he hoped it would earn him a fortune. Although the sax-horn did become popular, Sax never got rich, because he was a bad businessman.

PLAYING IN THE ORCHESTRA: A FAMILY AFFAIR

What do musical instruments and people have in common? Both come from families. Here's your introduction to all the members of the four families that work together in the orchestra—plus one member that visits often but remains in a class by itself.

Busy, Busy, Busy: The String Family

The stringed instruments make up the largest and busiest instrument family. They can laugh and cry and tremble, just like a human voice. All of them have strings made of wire, or cat or sheep gut. These are vibrated to create sound by drawing a bow across them. A bow has more than 150 horsehairs stretched between its wooden ends. To vary the pattern of bowing, players often pluck the strings with their fingertips. To make the sounds higher or lower they press down on the strings at the neck with the fingers of the other hand.

Violin. This smallest member of the string family rests its head against the player's shoulder. Pegs on the violin's neck can be turned to tighten or loosen its four strings. Because the violin has so many shades of expression, composers tend to entrust it with their most beautiful ideas and with many of the solo parts.

The String Family

Violin   Viola   Cello   Double Bass

Viola.   A viola looks like an overgrown violin, but its thicker strings produce a distinctly deeper, more mellow sound. The viola is an important team player, but only rarely a soloist.

Cello.   The cello has a full, rich sound and is even bigger than the viola. That's why it's held between the player's knees, propped up on a metal spike. For a long time it was considered the least important member of the string family, and few composers gave it important parts. It wasn't until cello players began to compose their own music that the "Cinderella cello" took its place alongside the violin as a star instrument.

Double bass.   Look in the back row of the orchestra for this giant of the string family and listen for its booming, bullfrog tones. The bassist either sits on a high stool or else stands, using a bow or fingers to vibrate the strings. Although the double bass is found in all orchestras, most pop groups prefer to use its cousin, the bass guitar.

Harp. One of the oldest of all the instruments, the harp can play the entire string family's sounds. Many modern players use electrified harps. Their music has caused quite a stir among those who associate the harp with angels and very gentle sounds.

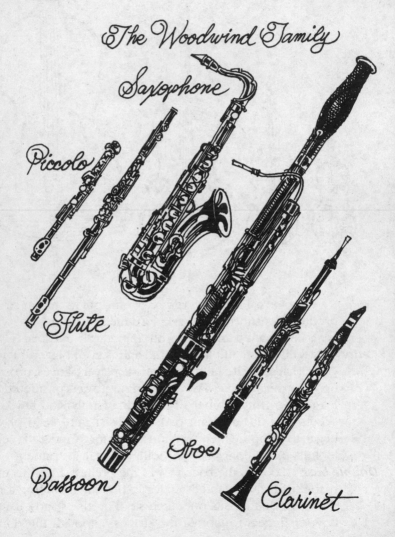

The Woodwind Family

Saxophone

Piccolo

Flute

Bassoon

Oboe

Clarinet

Howls and Squeaks: The Woodwind Family

When you listen to the woodwinds, you might think that they got their family name from the musical squeaks, howls, and honks they can produce. The fact is that they're named after the material from which most of them used to be made. All woodwinds except the flute are played by blowing air through hollow tubes called reeds.

Flute. A flute looks like a pipe, is held sideways, and has a sound range from deep and mellow to high and breathy. The instrument called a recorder is often used as a flute for beginners, though there are many advanced, long-time recorder players. The most unusual flute is the nose flute, which is blown through the left nostril.

Piccolo. This ruler-sized flute plays notes so high that you can pick them out even when all the larger instruments are playing. A big orchestra usually has two or three flutes, but only one piccolo.

Clarinet. The clarinet's great range of sounds makes it the most widely used and popular woodwind. It has a set of keys that are pressed to open and close its air holes.

Oboe. The oboe is a double-reed woodwind with a somewhat nasal sound. It looks like the clarinet but is longer and has a different mouthpiece.

Saxophone. This cross between the clarinet and the oboe started out as a military band instrument, but it has enjoyed great success among pop and jazz musicians. The sax has been a dance-band regular since the late 1920s.

Bassoon. Like the oboe, the bassoon is a double-reed instrument. It has a deep, husky tone and a sound tube that's almost ten feet long.

Blowing through Twists and Curls: The Brass Family

This group looks like a complicated family—all that curled and twisted brass! Yet these very turns are what make these instruments shorter and easier to handle. Because players create sounds by blowing air into them with their lips, brass instruments are sometimes nicknamed "blowers." To put it another way, the player makes the sound by blowing, then the instrument makes it louder.

Trombone. The mellow-toned trombone has been around in one form or another since the fifteenth century. You can move its sliding tube in and out to adjust the musical sound from high to low. When the tube is all the way out, the trombone is about three feet longer than its regular length.

Trumpet. The trumpet uses valves to change from high sounds to low ones. It became a popular jazz solo instrument during the 1940s.

Cornet. The cornet is a shorter version of the trumpet, with a somewhat less intense and brilliant sound.

French horn. Believe it or not, the horn started out as a long, straight instrument used by French hunters as a sort of two-way radio. Eventually, someone got the bright idea of making it more portable by rolling a brass tube into a round hoop. Once musicians discovered the many musical effects this design could produce, more and more twists were fitted inside the hoop. If you were to straighten out the modern horn's coil, it would stretch out to twelve or more feet.

Tuba. The tuba's heavy but lively sound is easy to recognize. So is its very wide mouthpiece, which covers most of the player's lips. Unwound, it would measure thirty-five feet! The *sousaphone*, named after its designer, John Philip Sousa, is a wraparound-the-neck variation for marching bands.

Banging, Booming, and Tinkling: The Percussion Family

The word *percussion* comes from a word meaning to hit sharply, and that's exactly how this oldest family of instruments is played. Some people call percussion instruments bangers, because you strike or bang them with a stick, your hands, or some sort of banger. Some boom like thunder; others tinkle or ring like bells. A few make rattling and scraping sounds.

The Brass Family

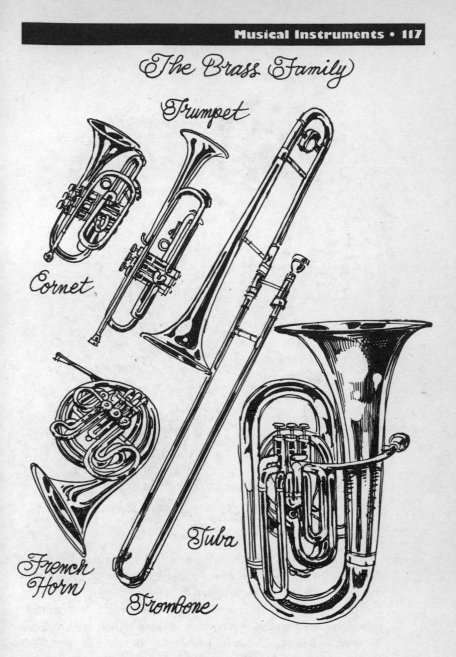

Trumpet

Cornet

French Horn

Trombone

Tuba

The Percussion Family

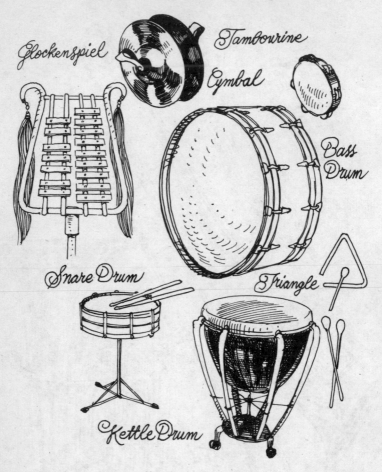

Glockenspiel

Tambourine

Cymbal

Bass Drum

Snare Drum

Triangle

Kettle Drum

Drums. Drums are usually made from a piece of animal skin or plastic stretched over an open-ended cylinder. When you hit the drumskin with a stick, a mallet, or your hands, it vibrates and makes a sound. *Bass drums* have very large cylinders that produce lower sounds than *snare drums*, which are smaller. With *kettledrums*, also called *timpani*, the skin is stretched over hollow metal shells and hit by felt- or leather-covered balls mounted on sticks.

Cymbals.　There's no mistaking the dramatic, crashing sound made when these round, thin sheets of metal are banged together. Very big cymbals, called gongs, are struck with a large, soft mallet.

Bells and bars.　This instrument group includes variously sized *triangles*, the *xylophone*, the *marimba*, and the *glockenspiel*.

Noisemakers.　Many kids make their own noisemakers to shake, rattle, and scrape together. Two favorites are *maracas*, which are dried gourds filled with seeds, and the *tambourine*, which has a ring of small metal disks around its edge.

A Player in a Class by Itself: The Piano

The piano is classified as a stringed instrument by some but as a percussion member by others. You see, when the player presses one of the piano's eighty-eight keys, a soft felt hammer strikes a string inside the piano. However one thinks of it, the piano is one of the most popular of all instruments. Because it's not used in every performance, the piano is not a standard orchestra instrument. However, it does play a regular and important role.

Grand

Upright

GREAT LISTENING FOR INSTRUMENT DETECTIVES

Here are some suggestions for enjoying music that will help you tune your ears to various instruments. You'll be amazed how easy it is to tell the difference between a viola and a cello, or an oboe and a clarinet. Recordings of the music and players listed below are available in most libraries and record stores.

A Musical Puzzle to Tune Your Ears

Don't let this long, complicated title scare you! Benjamin Britten's "The Young Person's Guide to the Orchestra (op. 34, Variations and Fugue on a Theme of Purcell") is guaranteed to turn you into an instant whiz at instrument identification. Britten, an English composer-conductor, created this musical puzzle from a tune by another composer. In Part One of the puzzle the whole orchestra plays the melody. In Part Two the tune is repeated, but this time with each instrument family playing by itself; first the woodwinds, then the brasses, the strings, and, finally, the percussion instruments. In Part Three the composer puts the tune he took apart together again. This time, instead of beginning as a whole family unit, the instruments come in one after another. (That's what the fugue part of the title is all about.)

An Instrumental Animal Fair

Any version of Camile Saint-Saens's "The Carnival of the Animals" is a wonderfully loony instrumental fantasy. The one narrated by Leonard Bernstein would be ideal to hear, because it tells you some of the composer's little "inside" jokes and has the Benjamin Britten "puzzle" (also narrated) on the other side. But with or without the storyteller, you'll be amazed at the instruments' acting abilities. There's the flute fluttering like birds, the double bass's elephant walk, the oboe crowing, and the cello's beautiful swan dance.

All String Quartets Are Not the Same

One of the most enjoyable ways to tune your ears to the different sounds of the violin, viola, and cello is to listen to any of the recordings of popular classical music groups like the Tokyo String Quartet, the Emerson String Quartet, or the Guarnari String Quartet. For a string quartet with a more contemporary sound, look for something by the Kronos Quartet.

For Virtuoso Watchers

Many supertalented players have made recordings with instruments that lots of kids are interested in. The music by the players on this list includes classical, jazz, and rock. You might also want to look up some of the players in Chapter 2 under "Today's Prodigies . . . Tomorrow's Legends."

Name	*Instrument*
Harry Connick, Jr.	Piano
Olfra Harnoy	Cello
Viktoria Mullova	Violin
Charlie Mingus	Double bass
Jean-Pierre Rampal	Flute
Richard Stoltzman	Clarinet
Branford Marsalis	Saxophone
Wynton Marsalis	Trumpet
Ringo Starr	Drums

Peculiar Piano Sounds

Imagine hitting a piano with your fists and forearms, or reaching inside it and strumming and plucking the strings. Henry Cowell, who lived from 1897 to 1965, was one of the first composers to use the piano in this unusual way. To hear what music played in this manner sounds like, check your library for the "Piano Music of Henry Cowell" on Folkways Records.

PLAYING IN A MUSICAL GROUP

You can put together an orchestra from many large or small combinations of instruments. Listed below are four common instrumental combinations. (See the next section for rock bands.)

Symphony Orchestras

Of all the musical groups, the symphony is the largest. The 100 or more instruments that make it up are divided approximately as follows and grouped as illustrated on pages 124–125.

Strings

34 violins, divided into first violins (the group closest to the conductor) and second violins
12 violas
10 cellos
8 double basses
2 harps

Woodwinds

3 flutes
1 piccolo
3 oboes
1 horn
4 clarinets
3 bassoons
1 double bass

Brasses

6 horns
4 trumpets
4 trombones
1 tuba

Percussion instruments

4 kettledrums

A glockenspiel, a tenor and a bass drum, chimes, a xylophone, and triangles, and cymbals

Five-Piece-Plus Orchestras

Small groups can create great music for both dancing and listening. Here are a few combinations that work well:

Five pieces. Violin, flute, clarinet, cornet, and piano.
Seven pieces. The five above, plus a cello and drums.
Eight pieces. The seven above, plus a double bass.

Chamber Music Groups

These groups can include from three to seven instruments. Some combine several instrument families. String quartets are especially popular (see "All String Quartets Are Not the Same" a few pages back).

Marching Bands

The Broadway musical and movie "The Music Man" had a song about a marching band with 76 trombones. But you can put together a very satisfactory marching band with just two trombones, some cornets and horns, and a tuba and snare drum. This can be expanded with a piccolo, another cornet, and a clarinet and saxophone.

PLUGGING IN

When you play an acoustic instrument the sound comes from the instrument's body. The thing to remember about electronic instruments is that they don't make any sounds until they're plugged into an amplifier and a loudspeaker. This electronically created sound can make a guitar boom as loudly as a drum and give a toy-sized piano a concert grand's volume.

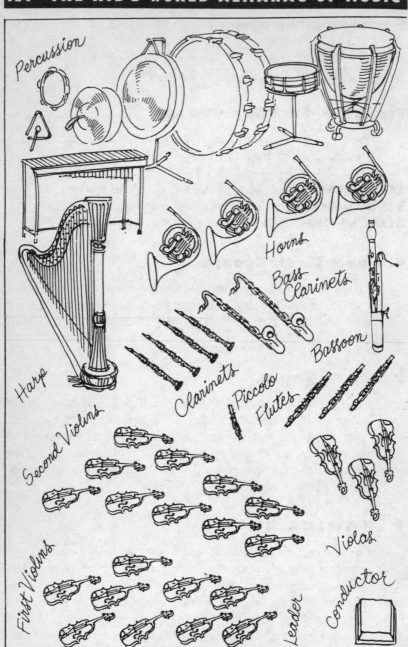

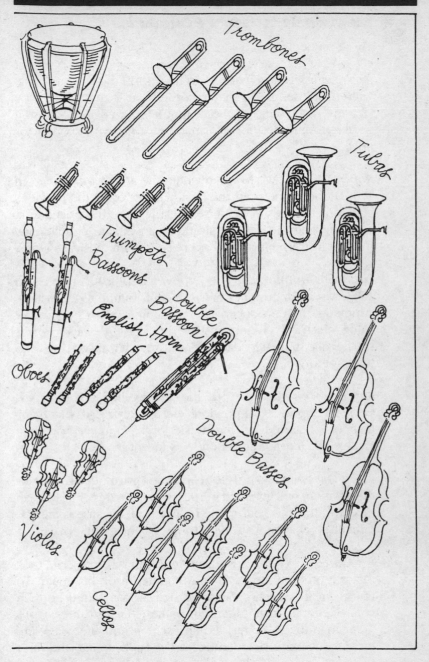

Trombones

Tubas

Trumpets

Bassoons

Double Bassoon

English Horn

Oboes

Double Basses

Violas

Cellos

Electronic Music's Pioneers

These pioneers paved the way for all sorts of truly amazing electro-phenomenon currently being developed. One of these setups is a powerful "orchestra in a box" system that will enable people to play recorded music that will not be "frozen" in the same form each time it is played. Instead they'll be able to interpret a performance just the way a conductor does.

Robert Moog. When he invented the *Moog synthesizer*, in 1965, Robert Moog put the best features of all the previous electronic devices into one reasonably sized and priced unit. This amazing piece of equipment can imitate virtually any musical instrument, as well as create its own musical sounds.

Laurens Hammond. The *Hammond organ*, invented in 1933, was an important American contribution to electric instruments. It reproduced the giant pipe organ's sound by using electrical circuits instead of pipes. Because it was smaller and more affordable, it pretty much replaced the original pipe organ.

Maurice Martenot. In 1928 the device called the *ondes musicale* so improved on previous electric keyboards that many composers started writing music for it. Its name was then changed to *martenot*, to honor its inventor.

Leon Theremin. The electrophonic instrument known as the *theremin* was invented in 1924, and named after its Russian inventor. It turned out not to be practical, because it was too difficult to change from high to low sounds while playing.

Les Paul. In 1927 Les Paul, an American jazz musician, took the arm off a phonograph and mounted it on his guitar. To transform the guitar's electrical signals into sound he then connected it to an amplifier. Since then this instrument that's older than the Bible has led an exciting new life. Many improvements have been added to Les Paul's guitar, the most

Some Electric Guitar Models

Gibson Flying V

Gretch

Supreme 40V

Gibson Les Paul

Steinberger Bass

Fender Telecaster

Strato-caster copy

popular of which is the Fender *Stratocaster* (named after its maker, Leon Fender). Since the late 1980s there's also been a lot of enthusiasm for the Paul Reed Smith guitar, also named after its inventor.

Thaddeus Cahill. In 1906 this Canadian scientist invented a contraption he called a *telharmonium.* It had a large keyboard and electric generators that swiveled around to produce signals. Unfortunately, this early synthesizer wasn't practical. For one thing, the signals traveled along telephone wires and interfered with people's phone calls. For another, it weighed two hundred tons.

THE ROCK BAND'S MAIN PLAYERS

Instrument	*How It's Used*
Electric Guitar	As a rhythm instrument to back up the singer or main melody, and as a lead instrument for solos and important melodies.
Electric Bass	Like the electric guitar, but with fatter and fewer (four) strings. It works as a foundation for a band's music.
Drum Set	As you can see from its name, this is a whole group of instruments:

- A large *bass drum,* played with a foot pedal.
- A *snare drum*, a *tom-tom,* a *floor tom-tom,* and a *ride cymbal,* all played with sticks.
- A *high-hat*—a pair of cymbals played either with a foot pedal or sticks.

AN INSTRU·MISCELLANY
An Instrument "Phone Directory"

Sometimes instruments are classified according to the way in which the vibrations are generated—by blowing across a hole (as in the flute), through a reed (the oboe), or into a cup-shaped mouthpiece (the horn, trombone, and so on,). Each of these sound groups ends with the suffix *-phone*, which comes from the Greek word for *sound*.

Name: Aerophone.

Explanation: Any instrument whose sound is produced by the vibration of a column of air.

Aerophone Instruments: Accordion, bagpipe, bassoon, clarinet, concertina, flute, harmonium, horn, mouth organ, oboe, organ, recorder, saxophone, trombone, trumpet, and tuba.

Name: Chordophone.

Explanation: Instruments in which sound is produced by the vibration of a stretched string.

Chordophone Instruments: Balalaika, banjo, cello, cimbalom, cittern, double bass, dulcimer, fiddle, guitar, harp, lute, mandolin, piano, ukulele, viola, violin, and zither.

Name: Idiophone.

Explanation: The sounds are produced by the body of the instrument itself stamping, shaking, beating, clashing together, rubbing, scraping, and plucking.

Idiophone Instruments: Bells, castanets, celeste, clappers, claves, clogs, cymbals, glockenspiel, gong, maracas, musical glasses, rattles, scrapers, steel drum, stamping stick, triangle, washboard, wood block, and xylophone.

Name: Membranophone.

Explanation: Membranophones create sounds by vibrating a stretched skin or some kind of membrane.

Membranophone Instruments: Bass drums, bongo drums, kazoo, kettledrums, side drums, tambourine, tympani, and military drums.

Nicknames and Abbreviations

Amp. Amplifier. A device to boost an instrument's sound; not an instrument in its own right.

Axe. Any instrument (originally only the saxophone).

Doghouse. Double bass.

Harp. Harmonica; used especially by musicians who play the style known as *the blues*.

King of instruments. Pipe organ.

Licorice stick. Clarinet.

Midi. Musical Instrument Digital Interface. A device, not an instrument, that connects electronic instruments to computers.

Strad. Much-treasured violin from the famous violin maker Antonio Stradivari.

Strat. Stratocaster electric guitar.

Squeeze box. Accordion.

Slush pump. Trombone.

Tubs. Drums.

 Instruments' Nationalities

Instrument	Country
Alphorn	Switzerland
Bagpipes	Ireland, Scotland
Balalaika	Soviet Union
Banjo	United States
Bullroarer	South America
Cimbalom	Hungary
Cheng	China
Didjeridoo	Australia
Gamelan orchestra	Indonesia
Guiro	South America
Gusie	Yugoslavia
Jew's Harp	Egypt
Koto	Japan
Mandolin	Italy

Instrument	Country
Mbira	Africa
Nihbash	Jordan
Rondolia	Philippines
Sitar	India
Steel Drums	Trinidad and Tobago

Famous Musicians' First Instruments

Bill Haley. The singer who recorded the first rock 'n' roll hit, "Rock Around the Clock," made his first guitar out of cardboard. When he was thirteen, his father bought him a real guitar, on which he entertained at auctions—for a dollar a night.

Jon Bon Jovi. When Jon was in junior high school he formed a band that met in his garage. They played on "air guitars" (nonexisting instruments), with records and the group's one drum and an amplifier. By the time he had written his first album Jon had acquired an inexpensive guitar and tape recorder, which he still uses as his lucky charms.

Fritz Kreisler. After this world-famous violinist and composer learned to read music at the ripe old age of three, he made himself a violin, from a cigar box and shoelaces. He then "played along" with his father's amateur musical group.

Dolly Parton. This famous country singer built her first guitar from a broken mandolin and two guitar strings, when she was eight years old.

Three Folk Music Favorites

Folk music refers to the vast treasure trove of songs passed along from generation to generation and country to country.

The instruments that accompany folk songs tend to be the kind that are easy to play and carry around. After you've looked through the two instrument lists that follow, check out the ones a bit farther down under "Five Super User-friendly Instruments."

Banjo.   The song "Oh, Susanna" helped to spread this six-stringed strumming instrument's fame and popularity. You can recognize the banjo by its long neck, round body, and bouncy sound.

Autoharp.   The autoharp is a popular school as well as country band instrument. It's played by pressing down on one or more bars with one hand while strumming strings that are stretched across a thin wooden box with the other. It can be held in your lap, on a table, or against your chest.

Piano accordion.   This instrument has a keyboard like a piano and also has a button board, for deep sounds and chords. The two boards are connected by a section of folding pleats called bellows. These are pushed in or out to create sound vibrations.

Kitchen Concert Makers

Spoons.   To play spoons (always refer to them in the plural!), all you need are two ordinary metal teaspoons. Place them back to back. Grab their handles with one hand and slap them back and forth against your knees. For variety, bounce the spoons once against your knee, then against your free hand, and repeat this.

Bones.   A popular variation of spoons.

Washboard.   Ever since people traded in washboards long ago for washing machines, folk musicians have given them new life as musical instruments. Strumming their ridges with fingernails produces a clack-clack rhythm that goes well with other instruments. You can probably find a washboard at a garage sale or flea market for a dollar or so.

Jug.   Before drinks were either bottled or canned, people kept them in clay and glass jugs. Today these jugs are the folk musician's tuba. They're played by blowing across the open top.

Wacky but Musical*

Tennis-shoe light walker.   Kelly Oliver made this percussion instrument by stringing tennis shoes and some Christmas lights on a clothes hanger. When the Light Walker was held close to the floor, the shoes banged against the lights. It made for a fascinating "sight and sound" show.

One-man band.   Tyrone Patterson created a woodwind and percussion band from a snorkel attached to the side of a wooden box. He can actually play part of Beethoven's Fifth Symphony on it.

Bass walker.   Antony DuRose hooked a rubber band to a wooden stick and attached it to an upside-down ice-cream bucket. He produces a twangy sound by plucking the rubber band. For the accompanying rhythm he bangs the bucket on the floor.

Paganini's shoe violin.   When the famous violinist Niccolo Paganini received a wooden shoe as a present, he hooked it up with four strings. Being a great showman, he then announced a special concert to feature five pieces played on a violin and five on a wooden shoe. No instrument maker copied his shoe violin, but it did become a collector's item.

Steel drum.   This is truly a case of recycling garbage into musical gold. The musicians in Trinidad–Tobago convert the

* The first three instruments were made by kids in a junior high school in Coon Rapids, Minnesota. These were featured in the magazine *Music Alive*.

local oil industry's large drums into "pans" that produce tones with an orchestra's sound range. The musicians carefully hammer the base of the drum into a concave or indented shape, then make deep grooves into the metal for the musical notes. These steel drummers have sometimes become world famous. Many recordings are available for those who can't get to Trinidad–Tobago to hear a live concert.

Glass orchestra.   A group known as the Canada Glass Orchestra actually performs on chiming, tinkling bowls, bells and bottles.

Seaweed horn.   Musician-inventor Bart Hopkins used kelp found on the seashore for his intricately shaped horn instrument.

Rock 'n' roll toys.   Do any professional musicians play on toy instruments? In 1987 a rock 'n' roll band called *Pianosaurus* became a big hit doing just that. Their Mickey Mouse drums, Smurf cymbal and plastic guitars and trumpets come right out of a Woolworth store's toy department. They've played for national television audiences and were featured in *People.*

Famous Amateur Players

This list doesn't include any United States presidents who played instruments. Why not go back to chapter four to check if any would be eligible to be added?

Name	*Claim to Fame*	*Instrument*
Woody Allen	Actor-writer-producer	Clarinet
Robert Byrd	Senator from W. Va.	Violin
Chevy Chase	Comedian-actor	Piano
Albert Einstein	Scientist	Violin
Benjamin Franklin	Printer-diplomat	Guitar, harp, violin
George III	English king	Violin

Name	Claim to Fame	Instrument
John McEnroe	Professional tennis player	Guitar
Steve Martin	Comedian-actor	Piano
Samuel Pepys	Author of famous diary of English life	Recorder and spinet

Four Insects with Built-in Musical Instruments

The trills and chirps with which some insects fill the summer air are produced with drum-like instruments that are part of their bodies. Most insect musicians are male and know only one tune, or at most a few simple variations. Their musical ability is inherited, not learned by practice.

Crickets. Crickets' wings scrape against each other so that they can "fiddle" with either wing. Most crickets keep the right wing as a bow. Some sing in groups. The males sing to attract females. By the time crickets come to the end of their life cycle, their scrapers are worn out.

Grasshoppers. Grasshoppers have a double set of wings that they rub from back to front to produce their clicking songs.

Katydids. These grasshopper-like creatures also use their wings to produce the one song they know. It goes like this: Ka-ty-didn't; she did; she didn't.

Cicadas. The singing of cicadas is limited to "tsh-ee-eee e-ou" in the daytime and "ah-o-oo" at night.

The Incredible Shrinking Organ

• When the Greeks invented the first organ, a few thousand years ago, they produced sound in it by forcing air through sets of large pipes.

- With the coming of Christianity, the organ became the most important church instrument. As religious life spread more and bigger cathedrals were built, and this naturally meant having more and bigger organs.
- By the year 1600, many organs had several keyboards, as well as a set of keyboard-like foot pedals.
- During the early days of the movies many large, gaudy theaters referred to as movie palaces were built. The palace fare usually consisted of a double feature plus a live performance played on a huge pipe organ between each show.
- Movies weren't the only places where large pipe organs were part of the entertainment. They also played sing-along tunes between innings at every baseball stadium.
- Today organ music is generated on a single keyboard. The silicon chip and the synthesizer have now replaced the pipe. They've shrunk the instrument, but not the sound! When you consider that the pipe organ had its origin in the portable pan pipes described earlier you might say that the organ has come full circle.

LEARNING TO PLAY

It's fun to listen to music—and even more fun to make music yourself. Here are the basic facts about what it takes to learn to play an instrument.

Six Super User-Friendly Instruments

Clarinet. The many keys and pads on a clarinet make it look complicated. The fact is, though, that they make the clarinet more flexible and easier to play than many other "blower" instruments.

Guitar. The popularity of rock and country music have made the guitar a top instrument choice for kids. This goes for both acoustic and electric guitars.

Harmonica. You can carry a harmonica around in your

pocket, pay for it out of a week's allowance, and learn to blow a tune after just a little practice. If you also learn to play the guitar, you can be a one-person blues band. Both Bob Dylan and Bruce Springsteen became famous for their wailing harmonicas and twanging guitar "bands."

Mandolin.   To produce this ten-string guitar cousin's beautiful, trembling sound the player plucks it with quick, vibrating movements.

Recorder.   This instrument looks like a clarinet, costs less than five dollars, and is as portable as the harmonica. It's also the easiest wind instrument for the beginner to learn.

Ukulele.   With just four strings to pluck the ukulele is one of the easiest string instruments to learn to play. In Hawaii, where the ukulele originated, the name means jumping flea. It may well give you a jump start on mastering other stringed instruments.

Seven Tips for Picking an Instrument

- Think about why you want to play. If you want to be in a band, instruments in the string, woodwind, and brass families offer the most opportunity.
- Listen to some music written especially for the instrument you are considering.
- Find out if it's taught in your school.
- If you're thinking about taking private lessons, check if there's a teacher in your area. If the teacher isn't within walking distance, discuss transportation and its costs with your parents.
- If you're still undecided, talk to your school music teacher.
- Pick an instrument you like, but make sure it's physically suited to your size. Also make sure that there's a place for it in your home.
- Carefully check out the list below. If you're gung-ho about one of the more difficult instruments, be prepared to work harder.

SOME INSTRUMENTS ARE HARDER TO PLAY THAN OTHERS

Instrument	Special Problems or Skills Needed
Viola, Cello	Both require more stretch and strength in the fingers than does the violin.
Guitar	The classical guitar's nylon strings are easier for a beginner to handle than an electric guitar's steel strings.
Oboe, Bassoon	These instruments are more difficult than woodwinds such as the clarinet and saxophone.
French Horn	You'll have to work just to get a note out of this instrument. All the brasses take more than just blowing. You must learn to develop the right "lip."

Six Tips for Buying Your First Instrument

- Try to get a musical friend's or teacher's advice.
- Go to your local music store and check out as many makes and models as possible.
- Try it out for sound and comfort. For instance, if you're buying a guitar, make sure your fingers can reach all the strings on the fretboard. If you're buying an electric guitar, listen to the sound quality at *low* volume.
- If money is tight, consider buying what's known as a school model to get started.
- Buying a secondhand instrument is another good bet for getting around the money problem. Because used models don't come with warranties, take an experienced player along when you go shopping.
- Consider *all* the costs. This includes the cost of an amplifier for electric instruments as well as bus fare, if lessons aren't available in your immediate neighborhood.

Eight Instrument TLC* Tips

- Even a small instrument requires care.
- Store it in a hard or padded case that is labeled with your name and phone number. Using the case is always important, but especially so during cold weather.
- If your instrument is meant to be taken apart after playing it (for example, the clarinet), do it.
- Keep it clean. Play with clean hands. Wipe metal instruments with a clean cloth to prevent tarnishing, and don't let dust collect in openings.
- Avoid accidents. This means keeping your instrument away from little kids or places where someone might accidentally sit on it or knock it over.
- Don't lend your instrument out casually.
- Keep it away from radiators and other very hot places.
- A good instrument deserves a checkup every few years. Do-it-yourself repairs can end up costing more than a professional checkup.

Answers to Questions Kids Often Ask

How do you find a music teacher?
If you live in a small town, your choice may be limited to only one or two. When you have a wider choice, speak to other students and their parents. If there's a music school in your community, find out if it's a member of the National Guild of Community Schools of the Arts.

My mother says that playing loud music will make me deaf. She's just saying that because she doesn't like hard rock, isn't she?
No. Electronic music, especially hard rock, is played at such high sound levels that many professional musicians have suffered permanent hearing damage. You can avoid hurting your ears by not playing your cassette player too loud and keeping the earphones near—but not directly on top of—your ears.

* Tender loving care.

However, when you play a loud instrument or attend a concert, the only way to soften the sound's impact is to wear earplugs.

Can you practice too much?

You'd better believe it. Leon Fleisher, who directs the Tanglewood Music Center, speaks from personal experience when he cautions students not to overdo it. He says that if someone had given him the same advice when he was a young concert artist, he would not have permanently injured his right hand. A good rule to follow is that if anything hurts when you play, stop. If anything hurts every time you play, see a doctor.

What's the earliest a kid who's not a musical genius can learn to play an instrument?

It's never too soon—or too late. Because he was convinced that all children have natural musical ability, the composer Béla Bartók wrote a series of piano pieces especially for beginners. And piano and violin teachers trained in the Suzuki method teach kids as young as two or three. On the other hand, today many grown-ups are just getting around to taking their first music lessons.

Can you play real music on toy instruments?

Most toy instruments are frustrating for beginners to play. Even experienced musicians, like the Velvet Underground and Seals and Crofts, have not had much luck with their attempts to perform on toy instruments. (For a single exception, also by experienced players, go back to the "Wacky but Musical" section).

Why is it called "Chopsticks"?

This famous piano exercise is played with two hands—either with a single finger or with both hands turned sideways as if to chop wood.

If you start out playing one instrument, do you have to start all over again if you switch to another?

No. Many musicians have played several instruments. The composer Johannes Brahms learned to play all bowed instruments, and also the flute and horn. At a time when the piano was considered the only instrument worth learning, Brahms was urging parents to have their children learn several instruments, in order for them to become more musical.

HOW MUSIC IS MADE

8

Music is a truly international language. Musical ideas are written down with notes and signs instead of letters and words. This notation system is understood by musicians all over the world. For this reason even a little understanding of how music is written down will go a long way toward knowing "the score" about the three basic elements of music: melody, rhythm, and harmony.

THE UPS AND DOWNS OF MELODY

- The musical alphabet uses only the first seven letters and repeats them over and over again: ABCDEFGABCDEFG.
- To show a melody's pattern, the notes are written on what

G A B C D E F G F E D C B A G

is called a *staff* of five lines and four spaces. The notes move across the staff, going up as the sounds get higher and down when they get lower.

- If the notes of a melody go higher or lower than the staff's lines, you can add your own *ledger line* for additional notes.

G A B C D E F G

- *Clefs* are two helpful landmarks found at the beginning of each staff.

  The *G clef* (also called the *treble clef*) is drawn so that the clef's circle goes around the G note's position. Once you know where the G is, you can find the other notes by reading each line and space on the staff and counting up or down.

  The *F clef* is also known as the *bass clef*. It uses a reverse C with two dots above and below the line on which the F note is located. Once you locate the F note, you know that the note before it is E and the one after it is G.

- A melody's sound is determined by the way groups of notes follow each other up and down the musical ladder. Most melodies arrange seven notes into one of two *scales*. The *major scale* gives a bright sound, the *minor scale* a sadder, more dramatic sound. Both scales take their names from the first or *key* note in a piece of music.

- Notes that move up and down the scale a full step at a time are known as *natural notes*. Notes can also move in half steps. *Flats* go half a step down, and *sharps* go up half a step. The flat and sharp symbols are placed before the notes they affect. If a note is going to be sharped or flatted throughout a melody, the symbol is placed at the beginning of the staff, on that note's line or space.

♭ *Flat — down a half-step*

♯ *Sharp — Up a half step*

RHYTHM: THE HEARTBEAT OF MUSIC

Rhythm Basics

- Rhythm is to music what a heartbeat is to your body. That's why the rhythmic pattern that's part of all music is called the beat.
- If you clap your hands so that each clap is held for the same length of time, you produce an even, rhythmic pattern. The musical term for this is to keep a *steady beat*.
- Beats in music can also be divided into various groupings (2s, 3s, 4s, etc.). Musicians call such groupings *measures* or *bars*.

THREE COMMON RHYTHM GROUPS

The Measure	The Pattern	Example
Two beat	ONE-two, ONE-two	Marching, walking
Three beat	ONE-two-three	Waltz
Four beat	ONE-two-three-four	Native American

What the Notes Tell You About Rhythm

A close look at the way notes look tells you how long to hold each one. Different notes, different beats! It's a little like dividing a pizza into smaller pieces.

Whole notes. These notes are held the longest, usually for four beats.

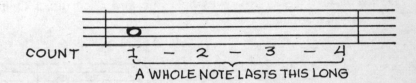

Half notes. These notes last half as long as whole notes.

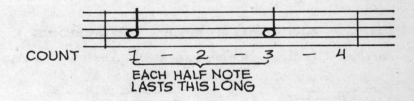

Quarter notes. Such notes last one-quarter as long as half notes.

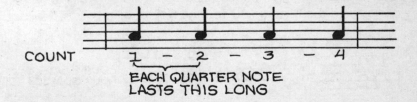

Eighth notes. These last half as long as quarter notes. Some don't have flags but are joined across the top.

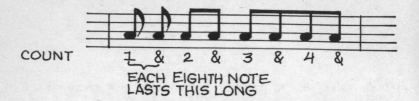

COUNT 1 & 2 & 3 & 4 &

EACH EIGHTH NOTE
LASTS THIS LONG

Dotted notes. These are notes held one and a half times their normal length.

COUNT 1 2 3 4 1 2 3 4

NORMAL NOTE
LASTS THIS LONG

DOTTED NOTE
LASTS THIS LONG

Rhythm-conscious Numbers and Symbols

Bar lines. These divide the measures. *Double bars* mean "the end."

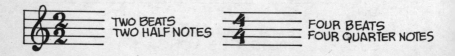

BAR LINE

DOUBLE BARS

Time signatures. These numbers appear at the beginning of the staff. The top number tells you how many beats in each bar, and the bottom tells you the type of beat.

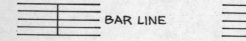

TWO BEATS
TWO HALF NOTES

FOUR BEATS
FOUR QUARTER NOTES

Curved lines or ties. These marks are used when one note is held from one bar to the next. (See the top illustration.) They can also join several notes in the same bar. (See the bottom illustration.)

NOTE LASTS THIS LONG

Rests. These show pauses in the singing or playing. These silent beats are held for as long as the note they replace.

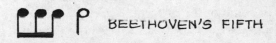

Five Facts about the Most Famous of All Rhythmic Patterns

- It sounds like this: ta ta ta taa.
- It looks like this:

BEETHOVEN'S FIFTH

- It begins Beethoven's famous "Fifth Symphony."
- According to music historians, the sounds were meant to give the listener a sense of fate coming to knock at the door.
- During World War II this pattern, which spells **V** in Morse code, was used as a victory greeting.

Test Your Note Know-how

You can probably sing "America" without looking at a written score. But reading and singing this familiar song is a great way to see how all this musical shorthand can help you sing or play any song correctly. The clef tells you that you start with the G note. The sharp sign is your cue to sing all the E notes just a half tone higher, and the time signature tells you that each bar contains three quarter notes.

AMERICA

MY COUN-TRY 'TIS OF THEE   SWEET LAND OF LIB-ER-TY

OF THEE I   SING. LAND WHERE MY FA-THERS DIED   LAND OF THE

PIL-GRIMS PRIDE   FROM EV-ERY MOUN-TAIN SIDE LET FREE-DOM RING.

FORM: THE MUSICAL PLAN

- Every piece of music has sections that have to be put to-gether in some order or form.
- Most songs have at least two such sections. The first, or "A" part, consists of a musical phrase that gives you the sense that you're going somewhere. A contrast, or "B" phrase, takes the melody to a complete stop. In the previous section you'll see this pattern illustrated in the musical score for "America."
- Many melodies repeat the first phrase in an ABA pattern— for example, "Twinkle, Twinkle, Little Star". Some, like "All Through the Night," repeat the first phrase three times in an AABA format.

ALL THROUGH THE NIGHT

A — SLEEP MY CHILD AND PEACE AT·TEND THEE ALL THROUGH THE NIGHT

A — GUARDIAN AN-GELS GOD WILL LEND THEE ALL THROUGH THE NIGHT

B — SOFT THE DROW-SY HOURS ARE CREEPING HILL AND VALE IN SLUMBER SLEEPING

A — LOVE A - LONE HIS WATCH IS KEEPING ALL THROUGH THE NIGHT.

HARMONY: MUSIC'S SUPPORT SYSTEM

In a melody, one musical tone follows another. In harmony, several tones or *chords* are played all at once. These chords are written one on top of the other on the musical staff (line-line-line or space-space-space).

TWO NOTE CHORDS   THREE NOTE CHORDS

"Phony" Music Making

Musicians refer to the way melody and harmony work together as *texture*. The words to describe the various textures all end with the suffix *-phony*.

Monophony.   This is musical texture at its simplest. Whether one or several people sing, it's monophony if each sings the same exact melodic line.

Homophony.   This technique adds more texture. Here one musical line takes the lead and all the other musical sounds serve as accompaniment to it. When you hear a folksinger accompanied by a guitar you're listening to homophony. The folksinger provides the melody, the guitar the harmony.

Polyphony.   Here you have two or more independent melodies, but they are more or less equally important. If you've sung a round like "Row, Row, Row Your Boat" you've sung polyphonic harmony. After one singer begins, the second comes in four beats later, and then a third might come in four beats after the second one. Each sings independently and is just as important as any of the others.

MORE MUSICAL SHORTHAND

The way music is played—loudly or softly, bravely or timidly, fast or slow—has a big effect on the feelings it stirs in the listener. Italian terms are generally used as the international language for these differences in what are called *pitch* and *tempo*. The abbreviations and words used for writing down music are also used on concert programs.

Pitch—How Loud?

The written signs for how loud or soft music should be played or sung are known as the *dynamics* of music.

Abbreviation	Italian Word	Meaning
pp	Pianissimo	Very soft
p	Piano	Soft
mp	Mezzopiano	Medium soft
mf	Mezzoforte	Medium loud
f	Forte	Loud
ff	Fortissimo	Very loud
<	Crescendo	Gradually louder
>	Decrescendo	Gradually softer

Tempo—How Fast?

Italian Word	Meaning
Largo	Very slow
Adagio	Slow
Lento	Slow
Andante	A moderate, walking pace
Moderato	Moderately fast
Allegro	Fast
Allegretto	Pretty fast
Presto	Very fast
Accelerando (*or* accel.)	Speeding up
Ritardando (*or* rit. *or* ritard.)	Slowing down

Taking the Guesswork out of the Tempo

Tempo instructions, unlike other musical notations, are not exact. Just how fast is fast? How slow is slow? A musical timepiece called a *metronome* can help you to be absolutely sure. You can set it at any speed to tick out the number of beats per minute. Here are some metronome instructions you might find at the beginning of a piece of music.

Metronome Marking	What It Means
M. = 50	Play quarter note at 50 beats per minute. (Anything up to 60 is considered slow.)
M. ♩ = 60	Play quarter note at 60 beats per minute. (Anything between 60 and 90 is considered a medium tempo.)
M. ♩ = 100	Play quarter note at 100 beats per minute. (Anything over 90 is considered fast.) U.S. army troops always march at a speed of 120. Music for dancing or at football games might sometimes go faster, to give more brilliant or flashier effects.

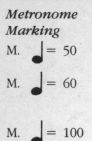 **NOTES FROM THE PAST**

• Long before our notation system was developed, people used to add little markers called *neumes* to the words for a song. If a melody went up, it would be marked with a short line going up (/). If the melody went down, the line went in the other direction (\). And if it went down and then up, the writer would combine the marker like this, (\ /).

• During the eleventh century, someone got the bright idea of drawing one of the musical staff lines in red and marking it with an F. This made such a hit that another-color line was then added to show the position of the G note. Naturally, these hand-colored staffs became pretty time consuming and expensive. Using the G and F clefs provided the solution to this problem.

• During the sixteenth century, people didn't limit themselves to using the staff we know today. In fact, some musicians went quite line crazy, with staffs of eleven or more lines! These big staffs got to be quite complicated to read.

• During the nineteenth century, a lot of singing teachers

experimented with variously shaped notes to replace the traditional *do re mí fa sol la si* syllables of the scale. To make fun of the many, confusing "buckwheat" shapes, one man even made up a joke scale of animal notes.

SONGS, SINGING, AND SONGWRITING

9

Did you know that the first pop singers to hit the road were called minstrels? And that Roseanne Barr wasn't the first "Star-Spangled Banner" goofer-upper? This chapter brings you a song bag of facts about the colorful history of songs and singers, from patriotic hit songs to the tops of the pops. There's even a section to help you write your own hit song.

SONGS LOST AND FOUND—IN CHURCH AND ON THE ROAD

- The first work song in history was the ancient Egyptian laborers' *shaduf* chant. It is also the only known song from ancient times. Because no one bothered to write down the other songs of the day, they disappeared as soon as they were sung.

- If early civilizations had kept track of their top songs and singers by their musical categories, religion would no doubt have been the biggest category. The Hebrew King David, for example, kept more than three hundred musicians busy singing and playing religious songs, many composed by him.

- Although church singing was extremely popular, it wasn't always very good. Singers simply chanted away, any old way they pleased. That is, they did until a bishop named Ambrose put an end to this free-form singing and came up with a specific system for chanting, which became known as Ambrosian chant.

- A pope named Gregory (590–604) improved upon Bishop Ambrose's chants. Gregorian chants quickly became the top chants of the day. Pope Gregory would never have believed that one day his rather somber songs would be transformed into jazzy dance music. But that's exactly what a group called Enigma did, in 1991. Their pope-to-pop album, called "MCMXC A.D.," became an international hit.

- As church singing became more and more important, even ordinary churchgoers began writing songs. In fact, there was a time during the twelfth century when every newly married couple had to give their local priest a special song on the Sunday after he had married them.

- For a change from the serious and formal songs performed by church musicians, people began to write and sing simpler, more tuneful songs. These early pop tunes became known through two types of traveling singers. The first kind, known as *minstrels*, or street singers, sang for their supper as they wandered from town to town and castle to castle. The other kind, *troubadours*, were usually born in castles. Love was both groups' favorite song theme.

- As more and more musicians came to roam all over Europe, singers in Germany decided to form a union of Meistersingers or master singers. These top singers were later made famous in opera by the German composer Richard Wagner.

- Many songs sung today are hundreds of years old. Because they have been passed along by word of mouth, from parents to children and country to country, most of them are quite different from their original versions.

- The earliest popular American songs generally had patriotic themes. Many were poems written to fit previously composed tunes.

THE OLDEST INSTRUMENT OF ALL: THE HUMAN VOICE

The human voice is much like a wind instrument. It works like this. The lungs supply the wind. The vocal chords set up the sound vibrations. Then the vibrations become louder as they pass through the throat, mouth, and nose.

Who Sings What

Singers' voices are classified according to the range of the notes they can sing. The musical notes for singers with high voices begin higher up on the musical staff than the notes for those with lower voices. What follows is a list of the female and male voice classifications, going from the highest to the lowest.

Female
Soprano.   The highest range.
Mezzo-soprano.   The sound range just below soprano.
Contralto.   A deep, mellow voice between soprano and alto.
Alto.   Same as contralto.
Male
Tenor.   The highest range. The only woman tenor in musical history was a Californian named Ruby Helderz.
Falsetto.   An artificially developed high voice, usually by tenors who want to go beyond the highest notes of their natural voice.
Baritone.   Deeper than a tenor, but higher than a bass.
Bass.   The lowest range.

 ## SINGING IN A GROUP

Whether its members are related or not, singing groups are like families. As in any family, some family members eventually go their own way or start new families.

Four Super Singing Groups

Group Name	*Members of the Group*
En Vogue	Terry Ellis, Dawn Robinson, Cindy Herron, and Maxine Jones are the latest in popular music's long list of popular female groups. In 1990 they broke into the big time with the hit song "Hold On."
The Jackson Five	The Jackson brothers were one of the most famous of the groups promoted by the Motown record label. The group consisted of five singing brothers: Sigmund (Jackie), Jermaine, Toriano (Tito), Marlon, and Michael. The backup singing or harmony was provided by sisters Rebbie, LaToya, and Janet. The kids became The Jacksons in 1976 and went on from there to successful solo careers.
The Supremes	The Supremes were another Motown record supergroup. High-school friends Diana Ross, Mary Wilson, and Florence Ballard were one of the all-time top girl groups of the 1960s. Diana Ross became a solo star, and Mary Wilson made a comeback after writing a best-selling book called *Dream Girls*.
The Jets	The Wolfgram kids were raised as entertainers. Each family member plays at least two instruments. They include Kathi, Rudy, Eddie, Moana, Elizabeth, Leroy, and Maiani. Another brother, Eugene, left to form a group called Boys Club.

Starr-born Teen Groups

The thing about teen groups like the Jackson 5 is that they grow up. But as one group grows up or splits up, there's always another one ready to rocket to the top. Since 1983, singer-songwriter-producer Maurice Starr has created teen singing groups faster than you can sing do-re-mi. The following list is in the order that the man called the General established them.

Group Name	*Members of the Group*
New Edition	This group started in 1983 with five teenagers between thirteen and fifteen: Ralph Tresvant, Ronald Devoe, Michael Bivins, Ricky Bell, and Bobby Brown. When Bobby Brown left to become a solo superstar, Johnny Gill took his place. In 1990 Johnny too became a solo chart-topper. The other guys regrouped as Bell Biv DeVoe.
New Kids on the Block	The fabulously successful Kids promoted rap dancing and singing among white teenagers. The original Kid and lead singer was Joe McIntyre. He brought in Donnie Wahlberg and Dannie Wood. Brothers Jordan and Jon Knight completed the team.
Perfect Gentlemen	Besides Maurice Starr's son, Maurice "Reese," Jr., this trio includes Tyrone "Ty" Sutton and Corey "Co" Blakely. These gentlemen were between twelve and fourteen when they recorded their first hit, "Rated PG," in 1990.

Group Name	Members of the Group
Homework	The first integrated, post-teen singing Starrs have family ties to two other Starr groups. David Knight and Melvin "Finesse" Sutton are older brothers to two of the New Kids and one of the Perfect Gentlemen. The other "Homeworkers" are Shawn Meadows, Raphael Deas, William Getchell, Diomedes "Dio" Aviles, Jr., and Evan Stent.

Superteen Stargazing

In January 1991 *SuperTeen* magazine editor Sharon Ginzler looked into her crystal ball and came up with the following list of three up-and-coming teen groups. The *Kids' World Almanac* consultants then added the Osmond Boys. In 1990 these Utah-born nephews of rock star Donny Osmond took a break from school to tour shopping malls throughout the country. The brothers kept up with their schoolwork by fax.

Group Name	Members of the Group
The Linear	This quartet features Joey Restivo, Charlie "Steele" Pennachio, and Wyatt "Riot" Pauley.
The Party	This was the first coed group to come rocking along. The partying gang consists of five former Mouseketeers on the Disney Show: Damon Pampolina, Chase Hampton, Albert Fields, Dee Magino, and Tiffany Hale.

Group Name	*Members of the Group*
Guys Next Door	After their successful 1990 debut on Saturday morning TV, the Guys—Damon Sharpe, Chris Wolf, Patrick J. Dancy, Eddie Garcia, and Bobby Leslie—cut a sizzling single, "I Was Made for You."

Chorus Line-ups with a Difference

Many singers get their first performing experience with a church or school chorus. The three kids' choruses listed below continue to provide their members with especially exciting experiences.

Choral Group	*Description*
Metropolitan Opera Chorus	Ms. Elena Doria prepares eighty-five New Yorkers aged seven to twelve to sing the kids' parts in operas performed at the Metropolitan Opera. Boys are more in demand than girls, but the chorus is coed. In fact, one of the most famous ex-members is a girl—pop singer and songwriter Debbie Gibson.
Harlem Boys' Choir	Dr. Walter Turnbull started this choir for inner-city New York schoolboys. Its 200 members aged eight to eighteen now go on world tours, make recordings, and are hired to do commercials. They sing everything from classical to pop music, but emphasize music by African-American composers. Most eventually go on to college and have nonsinging careers.

Choral Group	Description
Otawa [Japan] Children's Chorus	There has been an Otawa Children's Chorus for over fifty years. These singers from the Japanese village of Otawa Yurikago perform throughout Japan. In 1990, the current group traveled to Carnegie Hall in New York for a special concert for UNICEF.

★ **Who Am I?**

The singers in the dozen miniautobiographies below all started their careers very early. The names of the mystery stars are at the end, printed upside down and numbered to match their stories.

1. At twelve I sang in the London version of the hit musical "Oliver." Later I founded and became lead singer for the supergroup Genesis. Since I became a solo singer–songwriter I've had many hit songs about serious problems. My 1990 chart-busting album was, in fact, called "... But Seriously." It included "Another Day in Paradise," about homelessness, and "Heat on the Street," about racial tensions.

2. I'm one of fourteen children in a French-Canadian family of folksingers and began recording in 1983 when I was twelve years old. After four hit albums and fifteen Felix Awards (Canada's version of the Grammy), people started to call me the Canadian Debbie Gibson. To make my 1991 debut album, "Where Does My Heart Beat Now," I had to take a Berlitz language course. It all paid off, because the album zoomed right to the Hot 100, and the title song made it to the Top Ten Singles.

3. I began singing in my minister father's church in Detroit when I was nine years old and made my first recording at age fifteen. I've been a superstar since the 1960s. One of my big 1987 hits, "I Knew You Were Waiting (For Me)," was made with George Michael. Although most people think of me as a singer, I'm also a very good pianist.

4. I sang and danced on the vaudeville stage when I was only three years old. Although I'm no longer alive, you've probably heard me sing "Over the Rainbow" in the classic movie *The Wizard of Oz*. Two of my daughters, Liza Minnelli and Lorna Luft, are carrying on the family singing tradition.

5. My childhood in a New York City suburb was filled with musical activity: piano lessons at four, singing with the Metropolitan Opera's Children's Chorus, and writing and recording songs in our family's garage by the time I was twelve. When I signed my first recording contract, just before my sixteenth birthday, I became the first teenage star to write, produce, play, and sing her own music. One of my most successful albums was "Electric Youth."

6. I learned the ins and outs of recording when I was five by tagging along to my mom's recording sessions. At eleven I was singing gospel songs in my church choir, and during my teens I sang in my mother's stage act. I used my name as the title of my first album and set a record when I followed it with seven no. 1 hits in a row.

7. In show business the spotlight often shines on the baby in a family group. It sure did in my case, when I joined my four older brothers at age five. When I went out on my own, I became a superstar singer-songwriter. My video named "Thriller" set a record for the most Grammy Awards for one year.

8. Country singers often start early and remain stars for a long time, and I'm no exception. I sang on a radio show and made my first recording at eleven. Some of my most successful recordings include "9 to 5" (from the movie in which I played a leading part), and "Islands in the Stream," recorded with Kenny Rogers.

9. Chicago's my home town, and I've been singing professionally since I was five years old. I'm probably the only pop star who got started singing the praises of peanut butter and other products. This jingle singing was fine for a while, but what I really wanted was to be a rock singer and guitarist. This didn't happen overnight, but by the end of 1987 I was voted one of the Top 10 new artists of the year by *Billboard*, and in 1988 I had my first no. 1 hit, "Hold on to the Night."

10. I was born in Oklahoma, but I'm known as a California pop singer. In January 1988, when I was sixteen years old, I dropped my last name and became the first teenager in twenty-five years to have a no. 1 debut album, "I Think We're Alone Now."

11. I began singing with an English rock group during my teens, and people seemed to like my soulful songs right away. After singing with several big rock groups I went out on my own, in the mid-1970s. After a few years (no overnight success for me!), my singing career took off. Some of my biggest hits include "Don't You Know What the Night Can Do?" and "Roll with It."

12. I can't see, but I sure know how to make music. When I was only ten, I sang and played the harmonica on the streets of Detroit. And I was only thirteen when I recorded the first officially listed no. 1 hit, "Fingertips." That was thirty years ago, but I'm still a superstar.

SONG DIRECTORY

Name: Aria.
Definition: Solo song from an opera or oratorio.
Example: "The Toreador Song" from *Carmen*.

Name: Ballad.
Definition: A song that tells a story.
Example: "Barbara Allen."

Answers:

1. Phil Collins. 2. Celine Dion. 3. Aretha Franklin. 4. Judy Garland. 5. Debbie Gibson. 6. Whitney Houston. 7. Michael Jackson. 8. Dolly Parton. 9. Richard Marx. 10. Tiffany. 11. Steve Winwood. 12. Stevie Wonder.

Name: Carol.
Definition: Joyful holiday song, especially for Christmas.
Example: "Joy to the World."

Name: Folk song.
Definition: The general term for all old and usually simple songs. Most are by unknown authors, though many have been recorded by well-known musicians.
Example: "On Top of Old Smokey."

Name: Hymn.
Definition: A religious song of praise.
Example: "Amazing Grace."

Name: Lullaby.
Definition: A song to make a little child feel calm and sleepy.
Example: Brahms's "Lullaby"; "Rock-a-Bye, Baby."

Name: Nonsense song.
Definition: Song with silly, no-sense words.
Example: "Zip-a-Dee-Doo-Dah."

Name: Patriotic song.
Definition: Song to rouse patriotic feelings, often written during a war or as a country's anthem.
Example: "God Bless America."

Name: Round.
Definition: Song written so different singers sing the same song but start at different times.
Example: "Frère Jacques."

Name: Show tune.
Definition: Song written for a musical. Good ones are often remembered long after the show itself closes.
Example: "Tomorrow" from "Annie."

Name: Work song.
Definition: Special folk song written for or about people in particular jobs, like railroad and cowboy songs or sea chanteys.
Example: "I've Been Working on the Railroad."

What's Amazing about "Amazing Grace"

- There are more than 950,000 hymns in existence, but "Amazing Grace" is the one everyone knows.
- It's been a favorite hymn for African-Americans, even though its author was an Englishman named John Newton. What's more, he was a slave trader before he "found grace" and became a minister.
- According to the records of the Library of Congress, "Amazing Grace" has been recorded by more performers than any other hymn.
- It's been on the *Billboard* charts twice—as a recording by folksinger Judy Collins, and by the Royal Scots Dragoon Guards. It was also a best-selling gospel record for Aretha Franklin.
- The melody has been recorded in every musical style and performed at a variety of events. This includes concerts in prisons, by country singer Johnny Cash, and in Japan, by the Harlem Boys' Choir.
- The song grows and changes constantly as people add new verses.
- In September 1990 Bill Moyers, a television journalist, made a documentary and home video about "Amazing Grace" and the people who have sung it. This show drew two to five times more viewers than most public television documentaries.

Patriotic and Official Song Hits

Here Are Three National Anthems Everyone Knows
Anthem: "The Star-Spangled Banner"
Country: United States
Origin: Francis Scott Key, a lawyer, wrote the words during the attack on Ft. McHenry, Baltimore, during the War of 1812. He actually saw "the bombs bursting in air" and the flag flying over the fort at dawn. His words were set to a song called "Anacreon in Heaven," composed over twenty-five years earlier.

Anthem: "God Save the Queen" (or king):
Country: England. This song is often called the "anthem of anthems," because so many other countries have used the melody for their own anthems. These include Canada, Denmark, Germany, Sweden, and Switzerland. As "America" it almost beat out "The Star-Spangled Banner" in the United States.
Origin: It was first sung in 1745, but no one knows who wrote it.

Anthem: "La Marseillaise"
Country: France
Origin: Rouget de Lisle's stirring words and music were first sung during the French revolution, in 1792. The title was chosen to honor the soldiers from Marseilles who first sang it as they marched into Paris. Many composers have since used the anthem's beautiful melody. One of the most striking examples can be found in the "1812" Overture, which provides the musical fireworks for many Fourth of July celebrations. It was composed by Peter Tchaikovsky when his country, Russia, defeated the French emperor Napoleon. That's why the French anthem is loud and clear at first but is finally overshadowed by Russian music.

Star-Spangled Goof-ups at Baseball Games

• The list of celebrities who have sung the anthem during the baseball season is too long to list here. And so are the star-spangled disasters! These range from too much clowning around (Roseanne Barr), to humming and faking forgotten lines (Robert Goulet and Jefferson Starship founder Marty Balin), to just plain bad singing.

• To avoid star-spangled headaches, most sports leagues listen to tapes before hiring an anthem singer. The folks at the Super Bowl take no chances at all. Their singers lip sync the song to a tape. And in 1990 the people at Shea Stadium in New York bypassed using singers completely, by hiring violinist Itzhak Perlman. He may have agreed to play as an "opening act" because the great Babe Ruth once lived in his New York City apartment.

• Another goof-proofing technique is to use groups instead of single singers. That way if one fumbles, another can jump in.

• Opera star and baseball fan Robert Merrill holds the record for singing the anthem at more baseball games than anyone else. But even this star-spangled baritone once forgot the words.

• Many fans dream of singing at a baseball game. Jeffrey Wickstrom, a Seattle carpenter and amateur opera singer, was one who actually did it. He volunteered his services because he thought he could do better than some of the anthem singers he'd heard. Apparently the people he auditioned for agreed, because they had him appear at all twenty-six major-league baseball parks.

• Some ballparks play "The Star-Spangled Banner" one day and "America the Beautiful" the next, a practice praised by those who feel that "America" should become the anthem.

Anthems without an Official Seal of Approval

Many countries not only have official national anthems but also songs that portray the national spirit so well that they become unofficial anthems. Can you add any songs and countries to the list below?

Country	Song
Canada	"Oh, Canada" (also "God Save the Queen")
England	"Rule, Britannia"
South Africa	"God Bless Africa"
Sweden	"Sweden, Sweden, My Fatherland"
United States	"God Bless America" also "America."

Anthem Antics and Oddities

- Organizations and political groups often adopt songs that seem to fit their cause. There are two examples from the year 1990 alone. "U.K. Jive," by the Kinks, was adopted by the European Common Market Commission to promote its plan for a barrier-free Europe. And "The Ring of the Bell," by a Mongolian rock band named Hongk, was adopted as the new Mongolian nation's anthem.

- The Barbados national anthem was written by a Brooklyn musician, Irving Burgie.

- The Japanese song "Kimigayo" is the oldest as well as the shortest of all national anthems. It dates back to the ninth century and has just four lines. Of course, there are twenty-three even shorter anthems—if you count those without any words at all!

- The longest anthem in the world is Argentina's "Marcha de la Patria." It has an extended two-part prelude, followed by a thirty-three-bar verse and a seventeen-bar chorus.

- The longest anthem performance ever was given in 1900. The British King, Edward VII, had trouble getting into his uniform for a ceremony, so a German military band had to play "God Save the King" seventeen times without stopping!

States and Their Official Songs

- Twenty-five states have official state songs. Tennessee, which has one of the most famous, "The Tennessee Waltz," also has four others in its official song treasury.

- When African-American composer James Bland wrote the song that became Virginia's state song, he called it "Carry Me Back to Old Virginny." Virginia officials later changed this to "Carry Me Back to Old Virginia."

- Stephen Foster wrote not one but two official state songs. "Swanee River," also known as "Old Folks at Home," belongs to Florida, and "My Old Kentucky Home" to Kentucky.
- Alabama, Idaho, Nevada, Oklahoma, and Tennessee have official songs composed by women.
- Composer Paul Dresser wrote "On the Banks of the Wabash Far Away," the state song of Indiana. His brother, the novelist who spelled his name Theodore Dreiser, was rumored to have had a hand in it.

The Story Behind the U.S. Armed Services Songs

"The Caissons Go Rolling Along." U.S. Army
Edmund L. Gruber, a lieutenant in the field artillery, wrote the first version in 1909. John Philip Sousa then expanded it into "The Artillery March." When air power made the artillery less important, Dr. H. W. Arberg combined the two versions into one for the army's own song.

"Anchors Aweigh." U.S. Navy.
Charles Z. Zimmerman and Alfred H. Miles wrote this popular navy song when they were midshipmen at the U.S. Naval Academy. It was first sung when the Navy won the 1906 Army–Navy football game. Although most enlisted men take pride in the song, many consider it an officers' song.

"Columbia, the Gem of the Ocean." U.S. Army and Navy
Many people thought this song should have been our national anthem. Instead, it is known as "The Army and Navy Song" and used by both these armed services departments.

"The Halls of Montezuma." U.S. Marine Corps
You might not think of the tough Marines in connection with the opera. The fact is that their marching hymn is based on a military tune from a French opera called *Genevieve de Brabant*, by Jacques Offenbach.

"Army Air Corps Song." Army Air Corps
In 1939 the Army Air Corps offered a prize for suitable words

and music written for an official air corps song. The winning entry was by Robert Crawford, a student and vocal instructor at Princeton University. He became known as the flying baritone when he flew around in his own plane to give concerts.

American Wars and the Songs They Have Inspired

An army general was once quoted as saying that "a singing army is a fighting army." Songwriters have given the soldiers and sailors and marines and flyers who have fought in American wars plenty of memorable tunes to sing.

The American Revolutionary War. Although "Yankee Doodle" was not written for the Revolutionary War, it did become its rallying cry. By the war's end this song was a symbol of the Yankee as the new American. "Chester," by William Billings, *was* written especially for the soldiers and has sometimes been called an American "Marseillaise." It has had a long postwar life as a folk song, with more lyrics than anyone can count.

The War of 1812. Go back to the section on famous national anthems for details on "The Star-Spangled Banner."

The Civil War. Two of the best known of the many songs from this long and bitter war were "Dixie," written by Daniel Emmett, a Northerner, and sung by Southern soldiers, and "The Battle Hymn of the Republic," written by Julia Ward Howe, a Southerner. It was sung to the tune of "John Brown's Body," composed by Northern soldiers.

Spanish-American War. Patrick S. Gilmore, the official bandmaster of the Union Army during the Civil War, wrote "When Johnny Comes Marching Home Again" as a Union Army marching song. However, it didn't become a top marching song until the 1898 Spanish-American War.

World War I. George M. Cohan won a gold medal for his musical contributions to this war. They include "Over There" and "You're a Grand Old Flag."

World War II.   Irving Berlin's World War II musical "This is the Army" raised lots of money for the Army Relief Fund and British War Charities. The soldiers' favorite from the show was a pep tune called "Oh, How I Hate to Get Up in the Morning."

Korean War.   This was the first U.S. war without a single memorable song coming out of it.

Vietnam War.   Here's another case of not much to sing about. "The Ballad of the Green Berets," by Staff Sergeant Barry Sadler of the U.S. Special Forces, did become a big hit. However, it wasn't published until after the war.

Persian Gulf War.   This conflict set off a frenzy of amateur songwriting to cheer and support the troops. The professional songwriters' "musical missiles" included Bette Midler's 1990 Grammy-winning recording of Julie Gold's five-year-old "From a Distance."

Songs for Special Occasions

SEVEN PRESIDENTIAL CAMPAIGN SONGS

Song	President	Year
"Keep Cool with Coolidge"	Calvin Coolidge	1924
"Happy Days Are Here Again"	Franklin Delano Roosevelt	1932
"I'm Just Wild about Harry"	Harry S. Truman	1948
"I Like Ike" (From musical "Call Me Madam," with new words)	Dwight D. Eisenhower	1952
"High Hopes"	John F. Kennedy	1960
"Hello, Lyndon" (rewrite of the show tune "Hello, Dolly")	Lyndon Baines Johnson	1968
"Why Not The Best?"	James Earl (Jimmy) Carter	1978

SONGS THAT CELEBRATE SPECIAL OCCASIONS

Event	*Song*
Birthdays	"Happy Birthday" and "For He's a Jolly Good Fellow" (or "She's a Jolly Good Lady")
New Year's Eve	"Auld Lang Syne"
Valentine's Day	"My Funny Valentine"
Thanksgiving	"We Gather Together to Ask the Lord's Blessing"
Hanukkah, the Jewish festival of lights	Dreydl song
Christmas	"We Wish You a Merry Christmas," "Jingle Bells," "I'm Dreaming of a White Christmas"
Weddings	"I Love You Truly," "Here Comes the Bride." (Today's brides and grooms prefer pop songs of their own choosing to these once-traditional songs.)

 The Singingest Holiday of All

When it comes to having a long selection of songs to sing during a particular holiday, Christmas wins hands down.

The Nine Most Frequently Sung Carols

Carols are the oldest of all Christmas songs. They originated in England some five hundred or more years ago.

"O Come, All Ye Faithful"
"Silent Night! Holy Night!"
"Hark, the Herald Angels Sing"
"Joy to the World"

"O Little Town of Bethlehem"
"Deck the Halls"
"God Rest You Merry, Gentlemen"
"The First Noel"
"The Twelve Days of Christmas"

Three Song Facts for Your Christmas Stocking

- The first time "Silent Night" was sung, the organ broke down, so the singing had to proceed to the accompaniment of a guitar instead.
- "White Christmas," by Irving Berlin, is not only one of the all-time favorite Christmas songs but is the top-selling record in any category. The best-selling version, the one recorded by Bing Crosby in 1942, has sold more than 30 million copies. By 1987 the sales for all versions combined totaled 170,884,207—just for North America!
- Rudolph, of "Rudolph, the Red-Nosed Reindeer," wasn't always a song hero. Robert L. May invented him to star in a promotional booklet given to customers of the department store for which he worked. It was only after the booklet became a book that songwriter Johnny Marks got into the act.

It took a lot of persuasion to get cowboy singing star Gene Autry to record "Rudolph." He was mighty glad he did, though, for his record sold 17 million copies in one year. More than 100 other singers have since recorded it.

PLAYING MUSICAL GEOGRAPHY
Where's the Mismatch?

Each of the songs on this list is associated with a particular country. Do you know which one is lined up with the wrong country?

Song	Country
"Annie Laurie"	Scotland
"Alouette"	French Canada
"Frère Jacques"	France
"Juanita"	Spain
"O Sole Mio"	Italy
"Waltzing Matilda"	Ireland
"Yankee Doodle Dandy"	United States

Answer: "Waltzing Matilda" comes from Australia.

You Don't Have to See a Place to Be Able to Write a Hit Song about It

- Don Swander, who wrote the words for "Deep in the Heart of Texas," never set foot in the place.
- "Take Me Out to the Ball Game" is the official song of America's traditional national game. Albert von Tilzer didn't even see a baseball game until twenty years after he had composed it. And Jack Norworth, who wrote the words, wasn't a fan either.
- Walter Kent lived in California when he described England's coast in his 1939 song "The White Cliffs of Dover." He got his first look at the cliffs at the fiftieth birthday celebration for the song.
- "I'll Take You Home Again, Kathleen" is regarded as a typical Irish ballad. Instead it was written in Plainfield, Indiana, by an American of German descent who originally came from Virginia. What's more, he wrote it for his wife Jenny, but switched the name to Kathleen, because he thought it sounded better.
- John Howard Payne, the author of "Home, Sweet Home," was a wanderer who knew little about the pleasures of home. The song's melody was treated as a folk song until Payne could establish his legal claim to it.
- Stephen Foster wrote "My Old Kentucky Home" without visiting Kentucky. This is also true for "The Old Folks at

Home," also known as "Swanee River." When Foster needed a good two-syllable name for a song about a Southern river, he asked his brother to look for one in the atlas. He came across the Swanee River in Florida, which Foster then spelled *Swanee*.

NAMES WITH SONG CONNECTIONS

Girls' Names Featured in Famous Songs

Name	Song
Ann	"Annie's Song." From the musical "Annie."
Bonnie	"My Bonnie Lies over the Ocean." Nursery rhyme.
Billie Jean	"Billie Jean." Top hit recorded by Michael Jackson in 1983.
Carrie	"Carrie." A big hit for the group Europe, in 1987.
Georgia	"Georgia on My Mind." Recorded by Ray Charles, Willie Nelson, and others.
Jeanie	"I Dream of Jeanie with the Light Brown Hair." Classic ballad by Stephen Foster.
Ida	"Ida, Sweet as Apple Cider." Song associated with vaudeville singer Eddie Cantor, whose wife was named Ida.
Maggie Mae	"Maggie Mae." Rod Stewart's first no. 1 hit.
Michelle	"Michelle." A 1966 Grammy winner by Beatles John Lennon and Paul McCartney, and a successful remake in 1989.
Peggy Sue	"Peggy Sue." A fifties' rock hit for Buddy Holly that was heard by new audiences when his story was made into a Broadway musical.
Susanna	"Oh, Susanna." Another Stephen Foster favorite.

Girls' Names Featured in Famous Songs

Name	Song
Sylvia	"Who Is Sylvia?" Words from William Shakespeare's play *Two Gentlemen* of *Verona,* set to music by the composer Franz Schubert.

. . . and Six for the Boys

Name	Song
Alexander	"Alexander's Ragtime Band." The famous songwriter Irving Berlin's first tune.
Bill	"Bill Bailey." The most famous recording of this was made by jazz great Louis Armstrong.
Danny	"Danny Boy." This was a great hit for Al Jolson, whose life became a movie, and also for country star Conway Twitty.
Joe	"Joe Cool." This name comes from Charlie Brown and the Peanuts gang.
John	"When Johnny Comes Marching Home Again" and "Johnny B. Goode." An American marching song and early rock 'n' roll hit.
Jude	"Hey, Jude." One of the Beatles' no. 1 songs.

SONG FACTS FOR ANIMAL LOVERS

Chirpers and Peepers

- A bird's song is not just a single *cheep* or *peep*. Like any melody, it contains sounds that are repeated in some sort of pattern.
- The best bird singers are Baltimore orioles, bobolinks, canyon wrens, European skylarks, hermit and wood thrushes, purple and house finches, and nightingales and robins.

Some sing many songs, and bird couples often sing duets, with each bird singing different notes.

- Birds can sing as they fly, in the way a pop star can both sing and dance.
- Canaries not only sing their own songs but also mimic other birds' and humans' voices.
- The best melody learner of all is the starling. The composer Wolfgang Amadeus Mozart once kept a starling for three years, because it had learned to whistle a tune from one of his concertos.
- Sometimes things work the other way around. Ludwig van Beethoven's "Pastoral Symphony" ends with a passage that imitates a nightingale, a quail, and a cuckoo.

Five Rock 'n' Roll Singing Groups with Animal Names

The Crickets. This 1950s group was led by Buddy Holly, who split off to form his own band. All the members of this band died tragically in a plane crash.

The Beatles. This English group made rock 'n' roll an international music style.

The Byrds. This was one of the first folk rock groups. Their biggest hit was a song called "Mr. Tambourine Man."

The Monkees. Michael, Peter, Mickey, and Davy were the New Kids on the Block of the 1960s. They were the first group organized specifically for a TV series, which had been inspired by the Beatles. When it was discovered that the boys didn't play their own instruments, there was a big fuss. This was much like the to-do over lip syncing in 1990. The Monkees split up in 1969 but reformed in 1986, without Michael.

The Turtles. No, the Mutant Ninjas weren't the first turtles. During the 1960s the Turtles everybody knew were a pop-folk-rock group with a string of hit songs. "Happy Together" is known to this day. The group's leaders, Mark Volman and Howard Kaylan, still work together as disc jockeys.

SIX #1 ANIMAL TITLES FROM THE BILLBOARD TOP 40 CHARTS

Title	Singer	Year
"Hound Dog"	Elvis Presley	1956
"Puff, The Magic Dragon"	Peter, Paul, and Mary	1963
"Ben." The only top hit about a rat.	Michael Jackson	1972
"Crocodile Rock"	Elton John	1973
"When Doves Cry"	Prince	1984
"Turtle Power." The hit song from the Teen-Age Mutant Ninja Turtles' hit movie.	Partners in Kryme	1990

THE TOPS OF THE TOP SONGS

Each year the hits just keep right on rolling along. So here's a whole section of the tops in pops throughout the history of rock 'n' roll.

Yesterday's Heavy Hitters

All the songs on the next four lists reached the no. 1 position on the Top 40 and Top 10 charts, during the year listed. (A number of songs can be in the no. 1 spot during a given year.) Therefore, the songs on these lists were chosen from among several possibilities, based on the number of weeks they were in the top spot and how many of them remain popular oldies.

FIVE FROM THE 1950s

Song	Singer or group	Year
"Rock Around the Clock"	Bill Haley and His Comets	1955
"Don't Be Cruel"/"Hound Dog"	Elvis Presley	1956
"All Shook Up"	Elvis Presley	1957
"At the Hop"	Danny and the Juniors	1958
"Mack the Knife"	Bobby Darin	1959

FIVE FROM THE 1960s

Song	Singer or group	Year
"Are You Lonesome Tonight?"	Elvis Presley	1960
"I Can't Stop Loving You"	Ray Charles	1962
"I Want to Hold Your Hand"	The Beatles	1964
"I'm a Believer"	The Monkees	1966
("I Heard it Through the) Grapevine"	Marvin Gaye	1968

FIVE FROM THE 1970s

Song	Singer or Group	Year
"Bridge over Troubled Water"	Simon and Garfunkel	1970
"Maggie Mae"	Rod Stewart	1971
"Silly Love Songs"	Wings	1977
"Night Fever"	The Bec Gees	1978
"My Sharona"	The Knack	1979

FIVE FROM THE 1980s

Song	Singer or group	Year
"Physical"	Olivia Newton-John	1980
"When Doves Cry"	Prince	1984
"Faith"	George Michael	1987
"So Emotional"	Whitney Houston	1988
"Cold Hearted"	Paula Abdul	1989

Beyond the Tops in Pop

Rhythm and blues and country are the second and third most important categories in *Billboard*'s yearly ratings roundup. Here are 1990's top ten singles and albums for both categories. (Turn to near the end of Chapter 1 for the ten top pop singles and albums of 1990.)

Billboard's *Ten Top R&B Singles for 1990*

1. "Hold On." En Vogue.
2. "Make It Like It Was." Regina Belle.
3. "Real Love." Skyy.
4. "Feels Good." Tony! Toni! Tone!
5. "Vision of Love." Mariah Carey.
6. "All Around the World." Lisa Stansfield.
7. "I'll Be Good To You" Quincy Jones with Ray Charles and Chaka Khan.
8. "My, My, My." Johnny Gill.
9. "Ready or Not." After 7.
10. "Poison." Bell, Biv, Devoe.

Billboard's *Ten Top R&B Albums for 1990*

1. "Rhythm Nation 1814." Janet Jackson.
2. "Tender Lover." BabyFace.
3. "Please Hammer, Don't Hurt 'Em." M. C. Hammer.
4. "After 7." After 7.
5. "Stay with Me." Regina Belle.
6. "Back on the Block." Quincy Jones.

7. "Poison." Bell Biv DeVoe.
8. "Attitude." Troop.
9. "Johnny Gill." Johnny Gill.
10. "The Best of Luther Vandross' The Best of Love." Luther Vandross.

Billboard's Ten Top Country Singles for 1990

1. "Nobody's Home." Clint Black.
2. "Hard Rock Bottom of Your Heart." Randy Travis.
3. "On Second Thought." Eddie Rabbitt.
4. "Love Without End." George Strait.
5. "Walking Away." Clint Black.
6. "I've Cried My Last Tear for You." Ricky Van Shelton.
7. "No Matter How High." The Oak Ridge Boys.
8. "Help Me Hold On." Travis Tritt.
9. "Chains." Patty Loveless.
10. "Here in the Real World." Alan Jackson.

Billboard's Ten Top Country Albums for 1990

1. "Killin' Time." Clint Black.
2. "No Holdin' Back." Randy Travis.
3. "Pickin' on Nashville." Kentucky Headhunters.
4. "Garth Brooks." Garth Brooks.
5. "Leave the Light On." Lorrie Morgan.
6. "RVS II." Ricky Van Shelton.
7. "Simple Man." Charlie Daniels Band.
8. "Willow in the Wind." Kathy Mattea.
9. "The Boys Are Back." Sawyer Brown.
10. "Reba Live." Reba McEntire.

A SONGFEST OF TRIVIA QUESTIONS AND ANSWERS

Has a nursery rhyme ever become a popular song?
Yes, twice. Ella Fitzgerald made a big hit with a jazzed-up version of "A-Tisket A-Tasket." And Canadian folksinger Alan Mills turned "I Know an Old Lady" (Who Swallowed a Fly) into a hit song.

Is "On Top of Spaghetti" a folk song?
Yes and no. A group of schoolchildren in a suburb of New York got the idea for singing "On Top of Spaghetti" instead of "On Top of Old Smokey." Then the folksinger Tom Glazer rewrote their words and published this "new" song, in 1963.

Was there ever a real Waltzing Matilda in Australia?
No. In fact, the title of this Australian marching song isn't about a person at all. A matilda is a blanket roll carried with an Australian "swagman's" other equipment.

What was the song the astronauts in the space shuttle Dis-covery *heard on their first morning in space?*
"I Got You," a song with a long history. It was a big hit for 1960s rock star James Brown and also the inspiration for a rap classic called "I Feel Soul."

What are the oldest words of a popular song?
Turn! Turn! Turn! Composer-folk singer Pete Seeger adapted this phrase from the Book of Ecclesiastes in the Old Testament. It was no. 1 on the charts in 1965.

What song is called the cowboys' national anthem, and who gave it that nickname?
"Home, Home on the Range." The nickname comes from folk music historian John A. Lomax.

What was the first rock video to be aired on MTV?
"Video Killed the Radio Star," by an English group named the Buggles. It was on the Top 40 charts for over a year and a half before the MTV show aired it, in 1981.

What are the three most frequently sung songs in the English language around the world?
"Happy Birthday," "For He's a Jolly Good Fellow," and "Auld Lang Syne."

What songwriter has written the most no. 1 single hits?
Paul McCartney is credited with thirty-two. His former fellow
Beatle John Lennon comes close with twenty-six.

Whose songs have been recorded by the most artists?
This is another first for the Beatles. Their song "Yesterday"
has been recorded by more artists than any other modern
pop song, and their own version has been played more than
5 million times. Going back to prerock times, Cole Porter
takes the record for the most songs to be recorded by current
stars. These include the female rapper Neneh Cherry, Fine
Young Cannibals, k.d. Lang, Sinead O'Connor, U2, Tom Waits,
Aaron Neville, and David Byrne.

What are the best-selling pop albums of all time?
"Thriller" by Michael Jackson sold more than 38.5 million
copies worldwide. Fleetwood Mac's "Rumours" is the best-
selling album by a group. The best-selling album by a woman,
and also the best-selling debut album, is "Whitney Houston,"
by the performer of that name, released in 1985.

Janet Jackson made her album "Rhythm Nation 1814" *in
1989. Why wasn't it called* "Rhythm Nation 1989"*?*
Two versions have appeared in print: The explanation most
frequently heard is that the first letters of each word in the
title represent their placement in the alphabet (R = position
18; N = position 14). Another explanation links the number
to the year when Francis Scott Key wrote "The Star-Spangled
Banner."

THE INSIDE SCOOP ON SONGWRITING

Want to write your own hit song? Here are some rules and
tricks of the songwriting trade.

Seven Tips from the Pros

1. Remember that all songs, whether they were written by Stephen Foster or Stevie Wonder, have at least two distinct musical and lyrical sections, which are called A and B. For example, in "Happy Birthday" the first, or A section, is followed by a slightly different B section, then a repeat of the A section. Popular songwriters often vary this ABA pattern. Sometimes they repeat the A section three times (AABA). At other times they may repeat the two main sections twice in a row (ABAB). Some songwriters even use a third, or C section, which is called a bridge. The bridge takes the listener to a completely different place, as it does in the pattern that goes ABCAB.

2. Give your song a good catchy title.

3. Use the title at least three times, one of those times being at the beginning or the end.

4. A good lyric needs a hook to draw the listener into the song. This hook is sung on top of the part of the most hummable melody line.

5. Keep it short. Few of the world's standard top songs have more than a hundred or so words. "White Christmas" has 56, "Easter Parade" 76, "Rudolph the Red-Nosed Reindeer" 87, and "Over the Rainbow" 104.

6. If you want others to be able to sing your song, don't make the melody go too high or too low.

7. Don't trust your memory. Keep music paper, notepads, or a tape recorder handy.

The Most Frequently Asked Questions about Songwriting

Do you have to be able to read and write music to write songs?

Most songwriters do, but some don't. Irving Berlin, one of America's most successful songwriters, used a special piano that changed keys at the push of a lever. He took it all over the world with him. Today it's on display at the Smithsonian Institution.

Is it important to know how to play an instrument?
Again, most do, but many songwriters sing their songs into a
tape recorder, then give them to someone else to arrange
and write down.

What instruments do songwriters prefer?
The piano and the guitar.

Do singers have to write their own songs to be really successful?
The answer varies from singer to singer. Debbie Gibson does,
but Whitney Houston doesn't. Jon Bon Jovi and his band used
to write all their own songs. But it wasn't until songwriter
Desmond Child got into their songwriting act for "Shot
Through the Heart" and "Livin' on a Prayer" that they became
a superband.

*If you are going to write the melody and someone else write
the lyrics, which comes first?*
It doesn't matter. The lyricist Oscar Hammerstein II originally
wrote the words after someone else gave him the music.
When he worked with Richard Rodgers on the musical "Oklahoma," the words came first. Later the two songwriters used
whatever approach worked best for them at the time. Whether
you write the words or the music, you should know all the
parts that go into the whole. That way you can each help each
other if you get stuck on something. That's what collaboration
is all about.

Do songwriters make a lot of money?
Yes and no. "Happy Birthday," written by two schoolteaching
sisters in 1893, still earns about $1 million a year in royalty
fees. However, before songwriters got smart about getting
paid whenever their songs were performed in public, they
often sold them for a set sum of money. Stephen Foster sold
some of his songs for fifteen dollars. And Daniel Decatur Emmett didn't do much better when he sold his rights to "Dixie"
for $500. Keep in mind, too, that for every hit song there are

thousands that never catch on and even more that never get published.

What does it mean to sample a song?
Samplers are computer keyboards that can make digital recordings of just about any sounds. These sounds can then be played back through the keyboard and also changed and used with other sounds. Many pop and rap songwriters sample existing sound effects in this way into their music.

A Surprising List of People Who Have Tried Their Hand at Songwriting

The people listed below are just a few of the famous men and women who have written songs. All were accepted as members of the American Society of Composers, Authors & Publishers (ASCAP).

Name	*Main Profession*
Glenn Close	Actress
Clint Eastwood	Actor
Theodore Geisel	Creator of Dr. Seuss
Dustin Hoffman	Actor
Maurice Sendak	Children's book writer-illustrator
Lily Tomlin	Actress

TUNEFUL ODDS AND ENDS
A Colorful Hit List

All the songs listed below have one thing in common: their titles include a color. Can you add any other colorful titles? Or if you're into making your own trivia lists, how about song titles with the words "rock" or "roll" in them?

Title	Recording Artist
"Red Red Wine"	UB40
"Red Rain"	Peter Gabriel
"Under a Blood Red Sky"	U2
"Orange Crush"	R.E.M.
"Love over Gold"	Dire Straits
"Little Red Corvette"	Prince
(The Angels Want to Wear My) "Red Shoes"	Elvis Costello
"Blue Christmas"	Elvis Presley

Who's Out Front?

Every band needs a powerful singer. Do you know the lead singer for these popular bands? The list is numbered so that you can look up any names you missed, by turning the page upside down.

1. Def Leppard
2. Heart
3. Inxs
4. R.E.M.
5. Van Halen
6. White Snake

Song I.Q. Raisers

The best way to learn more about songs and singing is to listen and sing. The first three of the following suggestions are based on the Girl Scouts' requirements for earning a music merit badge.

1. To learn more about early singing groups like minstrels and troubadours, ask your librarian for recordings featuring songs from this period.
2. Learn a song for little kids, and teach it to a small child in your family or neighborhood.
3. Learn at least one song from another country.
4. Listen to an album by your favorite singer and see if you

Answers:

1. David Coverdale. 2. Nancy Wilson. 3. Michael Hutchence. 4. Michael Stipe. 5. Sammy Hagar. 6. Joe Elliott.

can pick out the main melody line and lyrical hook.

5. Try writing your own words to a familiar song.
6. Make up words and music for a silly song about something funny that has happened to you. To help you connect everything to the main idea, write down as many add-on things as you can think of. For example, for a song about a party make a list of the decorations, food, games, gifts and wrappings, silly things the guests did and said, and so on.

READING AND LISTENING

10

Get out your library card and check out some of the books listed in this chapter. There's something for every taste: from stories with musical backgrounds to biographies of great composers and big pop stars. And for all you baby-sitters, there's a picture book list to boost your rating with the little kids in your life.

MUSIC AT THE LIBRARY

Library Lore

- You can borrow records and cassettes just like regular books from most libraries.
- The Music Division of the Library of Congress is one of the largest music libraries in the world. It contains hundreds of thousands of copyrighted books and periodicals, records, sheet music, manuscripts by famous composers, and more.
- The Archive of Folk Culture at the Library of Congress has been collecting sound recordings, manuscripts, motion pictures, and photographs since 1928. A list of their records

and audio cassettes is available from American Folk Music and Folklore Recordings, c/o the American Folklife Center, Library of Congress, Washington, D.C. 20540.

- The New York Public Library at Lincoln Center is the only library exclusively for performing arts books and recordings. It stocks 100,000 books and musical scores, 11,000 items on the dance, and 42,000 records, cassettes, and compact discs.

- *Grove's Dictionary of Music* is the largest musical reference work. The latest edition contains more than 17,000 pages divided into twenty books, with almost 900 pages in each book. It features 22,500 articles, 16,500 biographies, 3,000 musical examples, 4,500 photographs and illustrations, and 9,000 cross-references. It took 2,400 people to put together this set, which costs $2,300.

BOOKLIST'S FAVORITE FICTION, FACT, AND PICTURE BOOKS

The lists that follow were compiled for *Booklist* by Barbara Elleman of the American Library Association and were adapted for *Kids' World Almanac* readers. Each entry begins with the author's last and first names, followed by the title of the book and the name of the publisher, plus a brief description of what it's all about.

Stories with Musical Twists

Angell, Judie. *Buffalo Nickel Blues Band.* Bradbury. Eddie and his friends struggle to establish their band.

Duder, Tessa. *Jellybean.* Viking. Even though she resents her mother's dedication to the cello, Jellybean wants to be an orchestra conductor.

Gilson, Jamie. *Dial Leroi Rupert.* Lothrop. When Mitch and his friends break someone's window, a disc jockey helps them earn money to pay for its repair.

Hilgartner, Beth. A *Murder for Her Majesty.* Houghton Mifflin. A girl in sixteenth-century England disguises herself as one of the York Minster Choir Boys after she sees her father murdered.

Le Guin, Ursula. Very Far Away from Anything Else. Macmillan. Natalie, a serious musician, and intellectually gifted Owen struggle to follow their dreams and deal with problems in their relationships with each other and their families.

McCaffrey, Anne. Dragonsong. Macmillan. Menolly is the first girl to be trained as a harpist at Harper Hall. Her story takes place in the dragon-filled fantasy land of Fern.

Newton, Suzanne. I Will Call It Georgie's Blues. Viking. Neal's ambition to be a jazz musician helps him through a family crisis.

Paterson, Katherine. Come Sing, Jimmy Jo. Dutton. Eleven-year-old James faces the pleasures and problems of being the featured singer in his family's suddenly successful country music group.

Showell, Ellen. Cecelia and the Blue Mountain Boy. Lothrop. Cecelia runs away from her bleak Appalachian town and finds Blue Mountain. She also finds a fiddler boy who shares her love of music.

Tarleton, Gillian Leigh. Two Worlds of Coral Harper. Harcourt Brace Jovanovich. Music sustains Coral when her life is turned upside down after her mother's death.

Weller, Frances Ward. Boat Song. Macmillan. Eleven-year-old James gets help from a Scottish bagpiper in communicating with his father. He also comes to love the man's music.

A Bookbag of Music Information

Anderson, David. The Piano Makers. Pantheon. A step-by-step photographic tour through the manufacture of a Steinway piano.

Arnold, Caroline. Music Lessons for Alex. Clarion. A photo-illustrated account showing a violin student selecting an instrument, taking her first lesson, and practicing at home.

Bierhorst, John. A Cry from the Earth: Music of the North American Indians. Macmillan/Four Winds. A history of the part music has played in the lives of Native Americans, with many examples of their music.

Englander, Roger. *Opera! What's All the Screaming About?* Walker. An inside look at the opera, along with the stories of fifty of the most familiar ones.

English, Betty Lou. *You Can't Be Timid with a Trumpet.* Lothrop. Behind the scenes with a symphony orchestra, giving an in-depth look at each instrument. It includes photos of and conversations with the players.

Fornatale, Pete. *The Story of Rock 'n' Roll.* Morrow. Here's a book all about rock, from the beginning to the 1970s.

Powers, Bill. *Behind the Scenes of a Broadway Musical.* Crown. Maurice Sendak's character Really Rosie introduces you to the whole cast of people involved in putting on a musical show.

Schaaf, Peter. *The Violin Close-Up.* Macmillan/Four Winds. Photographs with brief explanations show the violin from all its angles.

Walther, Tom. *Make Mine Music.* Little, Brown. If you're interested in making and playing your own musical instrument, here's a guide to help you do it. Two more possibilities suggested by the *Kids' World Almanac* consultants were:

Anders, Rebecca. *Making Musical Instruments.* Lerner.
Wiseman, Ann. *Improvised Instruments.* Scribners.

Ten for Big Kids to Read to Little Kids

Carlson, Nancy. *Loudmouth George and the Cornet.* Carolrhoda. Loudmouth George is a rabbit who brags that he's a virtuoso on the cornet. He gets his comeuppance when he joins the school band. If they like this one, look also for *Harriet's Recital*, by the same author and publisher.

Hasley, Dennis. *The Old Banjo.* Macmillan. A fantasy about a farm boy and his father who are called home from the fields by the sounds of a self-playing banjo, a trombone, and an old piano.

Isle, Elizabeth. *Pooks.* Lippincott. The story of real-life cellist and conductor Mstislav Rostropovich and his small dog Pooks.

Komaiko, Leah. *I Like the Music.* Harper. A little girl discovers that symphony music is as much fun as street music when her grandmother takes her to an outdoor concert.

Kuskin, Karla. *The Philharmonic Gets Dressed*. Harper. Follow the 105 members of an orchestra from the time they get dressed to the time they take their places on stage.

Martin, Bill, and Archambault, John. *Barn Dance*. Holt. A skinny kid joins a fiddling scarecrow and the farm animals in a barn dance under the light of the full moon.

Thomas, Ianthe. *Willie Blows a Mean Horn*. Harper. A young boy dreams of the day when people will love his music as they do that of his father, Willie the Jazz King.

Tusa, Tricia. *Miranda*. Macmillan. Miranda loves to play the piano, but she's torn between playing the great composers and boogie woogie.

Walter, Mildred P. *Ty's One-Man Band*. Macmillan/Four Winds. A young boy discovers the pleasures of a one-man band from a mysterious peg-legged man who makes music with a washbasin, a pail, spoons, and a comb.

Williams, Vera. *Music Is for Everyone*. Greenwillow. Rosa organizes the Oak Street Band to play for neighborhood parties, to pay her Grandma's medical bills.

MUSICAL LIVES
A Sampler of Biographies

Brown, Gene. *Duke Ellington*. Silver Burdett. The story of the great jazz pianist.

Ewen, David. *The Cole Porter Story*. Holt. The life story of the songwriter known as the elegant Hoosier.

Goffstein, M. B. *A Little Schubert*. Godine. This book is especially good for music students, because it includes easy-to-play arrangements of some of the composer's waltzes.

Greenfield, Eloise. *Paul Robeson*. Crowell. This work covers the African-American singer's musical and political life.

Holst, Imogene. And other authors. *Bach*. Garden City. One in a series about great composers.

Kaufmann, Helen L. *The Story of Sergei Prokofiev*. Lippincott. Another good "great composer" biography.

Nichols, Janet. *American Music Makers*. Walker. Ten biographies rolled into one fascinating book. The connecting link is that all the musicians are twentieth-century composers.

Sive, Helen R. *Music's Connecticut Yankee*—Charles Ives. Atheneum. Find out how this composer combined a career in business with music.

Pops in Print

When a pop musician's name seems to be glued to the tops of the charts, you can bet your favorite album that writers will rush to their computers to prepare that star's biography. (If that star is a teen fave, you can bet *two* albums.) The list that follows includes several books about musical styles, plus one for would-be pop songwriters. Titles with an * are paperbacks.

Greenberg, Keith Elliot. *Madonna*. Lerner. The blonde singer-dancer from the beginning to around 1985.

Greenberg, Keith Elliot. *Rap*. Lerner. The whole rap—from the early inner-city street rappers to the first Rap Grammy award (for "Bust a Move," by Young M. C.). Because this was published when rap was just starting to rock the music world, it doesn't include the 1990s rappers.

Greenberg, Keith Elliot. *Whitney Houston*. Lerner. If you enjoy this author's profiles of Madonna (above) and Whitney, look for his books about Cindy Lauper and Bruce Springsteen.

Jackson, Michael. *Moonwalk*. Doubleday. Several Jackson biographies are available, but this one is from the superstar's own lips.

Joseph, Jonathan, Donnie, Danny and Jordan. *Our Story: New Kids on the Block*.* Bantam. At one point during 1990 there were three best-selling books about this supergroup. Finally, the Kids decided to come out with their own story. Other Block-busters range from a $25 album by Lynn Goldsmith to less-than-$4 paperbacks.

Krishef, Robert K., and Lake, Bonnie. *Western Stars of Country Music*. Lerner. A nice introduction to the established stars of country music.

Krishef, Robert K. *Dolly Parton*. Lerner. Besides this actress-singer's story this author has also written *Jimmie Rodgers, The New Breed*, and *The Grand Ole Opry*.

Krulik, Nancy E.   *M. C. Hammer & Vanilla Ice: The Hip-Hop Never Stops.** Scholastic. This slim 76-page volume tells the story of the two superstars of rap 'n' pop. The same author and publisher also did a New Kids book.

Liggett, Mark and Cathy.   *The Complete Handbook of Songwriting.** NAL/Plume. The inside scoop for would-be pop songwriters, from how to do it to how to get your songs produced.

Mabery, D. L.   *Janet Jackson.* Lerner. Lots of photos, including some in color. By the same author and publisher are *Julian Lennon, This is Michael Jackson,* and *Tina Turner.*

Reisfeld, Randi.   *Debbie Gibson: Electric Star.** Bantam/Starfire. The second part of the title is a tie-in to this pop queen's *Electric Youth* album. By the time you read this book, another title in this series should be available in your local bookstore: *Nelson,* about the metal music twins with the beautiful blonde hair.

Watkins, William H., and Franklin, Eric N.   *Breakdance.** Contemporary. The rap explosion began with breakdancing, and you'll recognize many still-used routines. When you flip this nifty little book from front to back the photos in the corner of each page become a breakdance performance.

SONGBOOKS

All the songbooks and cassettes listed below (except the song cassette) include scores that are easy enough for beginning piano and guitar players to play.

Lobel, Anita.   *Singing Bee! A Collection of Favorite Children's Songs.* Lothrop. Here are 125 songs, plus colorful illustrations.

Nelson, Esther.   *The Silly Songbook* and *The World's Best Funny Songs.* Sterling. If you love familiar songs with zany new lyrics, you'll love these books. If your library doesn't carry the go-along cassettes, write to Dimension 5, Box 403, Kingsbridge Station, Bronx, NY 10463.

Nelson, Esther.   *Musical Games.* Sterling. Musical games for one to twenty players. Super for parties.

Nelson, Esther.   *The Great Round Song Book.* Sterling. A whole book of rounds. The familiar ones like "Frère Jacques" and

"Three Blind Mice," are here, as well as lots that you've probably never heard before.

Sharon, Lois and Bran. *Song Cassettes*. These fun cassettes don't come with a book, but they do have a fold-out sheet with all the words.

MUSICAL FUN AND ACTIVITIES

A *Kids' World Almanac* questionnaire distributed to three thousand fifth-grade students found that "taking a trip" rated tops as "the happiest moment of the past year." Kids also love to collect things related to their special interests. And so this chapter. It will guide you to the tops in musical sights and events, plus suggest lots of music-related collectibles and fun things you can do without leaving home.

ON THE MUSIC TRAIL
A Miniguide to Summer Festivals

Summer is barbecue, ballgame, and swim season. It's also a time when the sound of music fills the air. Festivals of all kinds are held in city and country settings, in the United States and other parts of the world. Here are some of the best festivals. Check your local newspaper for the ones nearest you. And contact the Chamber of Commerce in towns you plan to visit, to find out about others and their exact dates.

Asheville Mountain Dance and Folk Festival, Asheville, N.C.

This August event began in 1928 to preserve mountain music. It is the oldest American folk and dance festival.

Aspen Music Festival, Aspen, Colo.

Set in a picturesque Rocky Mountain resort town, this festival runs from the last week in June until the third week in August. Festival visitors have a choice of classical concerts by well-known composers and talented students from the summer music school.

Eisteddfod Festival of Traditional Music and Crafts, Southeastern Massachusetts University, North Dartmouth, Mass.

The name *Eisteddfod* is a Welsh word for "the coming together of minstrels." That's exactly what this festival is all about. Singers and musicians of all ages bring dulcimers, bagpipes, and other instruments to become part of the fun. The festival takes place in late September and lasts for three days.

Flagstaff Summer Festival, Flagstaff, Ariz.

Flagstaff's festival takes place from June through July. It features musical and theater events and special children's festivals.

Freiberg Tent Music Festival, Freiburg, Germany

Europe has many music festivals, but the Freiberg festival is in a class by itself. Its many tents are filled with all types of music, from classical recitals to singing clowns and rock groups.

W. C. Handy Music Festival, Florence, Ala.

Jazz great W. C. Handy would enjoy this annual August celebration in his native town. A very special feature is an "ABC's of Jazz" program for children.

Heritage Jazz Festival, New Orleans, La.

For two weekends in May the New Orleans fairgrounds turn into the Jazz and Heritage Festival, better known as the Jazzfest. Tens of thousands of people listen to overlapping sets of brass-band music, jazz, blues, rock, Carribean music, rhythm and blues, zydeco (a type of dance music that combines Carribean music with rhythm and blues and stars the accordion), Mardi Gras Indian chants, country, Cajun music, African rock—and yes, rap! In 1995 the Jazzfest will celebrate its twenty-fifth anniversary.

Hollywood Bowl Summer Series, Hollywood, Calif.

The best deals for kids during the annual Hollywood Bowl concerts are the daytime open house at the Hollywood Bowl events and the Children's Early Evening Concerts.

Interlochen National Music Camp, Interlochen, Mich.

This is the largest—and oldest—music camp for young people in the entire United States. From the last week in June through the last week in August, more than 1,500 students from every state and more than a dozen foreign countries come to this beautiful northern Michigan setting to make music and art. They range in age from eight years old to college age. The public is invited to many free student concerts. For a schedule and a list of places to stay, write to the National Music Camp, Interlochen, MI 49643 or to the Traverse City Chamber of Commerce, Box 387, Traverse City, MI 49684.

International Festival of the Arts, Dunseith, N. D.

Each year Dunseith and the neighboring Canadian province of Manitoba organize this six-week festival at the beautiful International Peace Gardens. The music ranges from classical to country and western to band music. It all happens in June and July.

Mystic Seaport Music Festival, Mystic, Conn.

Mystic Seaport in eastern Connecticut is a popular travel stop at any time, but especially so in June. That's when you can hear authentic sea chanteys performed.

National Old Time Fiddlers' Contest, Weiser, Id.

If you like fiddlers, come to Weiser in June for a week of nonstop fiddling. The more than three hundred fiddlers are between the ages of three and ninety-two and come from thirty states as well as Canada.

Old Time Fiddler's Jamboree, Smithfield, Tenn.

July Fourth is a big day in this small town. Everybody who plays a folk instrument participates in concerts and contests all over the place. For super fun there's a novelty instrument concert.

Peter Britt Festival, Jacksonville, Ore.

This jazz, bluegrass, and musical theater festival takes place in a beautiful setting. It starts in late June and lasts to the end of August.

Ravinia Festival, Chicago, Ill.

For eleven weeks each summer the Chicago Symphony fills the air of Ravinia Park with beautiful music. The performances feature leading soloists and conductors, as well as young musicians attending the Young Artists' Institute.

Saratoga Performing Arts Center, Saratoga Springs, N. Y., Dance Museum.

Enjoy the best in classical and rock music and ballet, plus a fascinating dance museum.

Spoleto Festival U.S.A., Charleston, S.C.

This festival was started to form a musical link between the United States and the music-oriented city of Spoleto, Italy. The summer's festivities end with Spoleto's Finale Orchestral Concert and a brilliant fireworks display.

Tanglewood Festivals, Lenox, Mass.
The lush Berkshire Mountains are the backdrop for two months of concerts. The chief music makers are the Boston Symphony, students of the Tanglewood Institute, and Boston's Young Artists' Institute plus many guest performers. The most fun day of the whole summer is Tanglewood Day, in mid-August. It features unusual instrument demonstrations and music all over the place, from 2:00 P.M. to an evening finale with fireworks.

AMERICAN CITIES AND THE SPECIAL MUSIC ASSOCIATED WITH THEM

City	*Music*
Asheville	Appalachian mountain music
Chicago	Jazz and early rock
Detroit	Motown Records and the Motown sound
Memphis	Blues
Nashville	Country
New Orleans	Jazz
New York	Broadway musicals
St. Louis	Ragtime

Musical Sightseeing

Stephen Foster State Folk Culture Center, White Springs, Fla.
This center, located on the Suwannee River, displays dioramas of scenes from Stephen Foster's most famous songs. A festival of traditional music celebrates his memory every May.

Graceland, Memphis, Tenn.
This is the mansion where Elvis Presley, the king of rock 'n' roll, lived. The king's clothing, jewels, guitars, and other memorabilia are on display.

Liberace Museum, Las Vegas, Nev.

The pianist Liberace was as famous for his rhinestone-studded costumes, cars, and pianos as for his music. This museum is a showcase of the glitziest and glossiest of the lot. If you go, don't miss the miniature pianos.

Lincoln Center, New York, N.Y.

This giant entertainment complex is located in the heart of New York City. It offers fascinating backstage tours of the Metropolitan Opera and other Lincoln Center theaters. The gift shop on the subway level is a favorite kids' stop.

Luray Caverns, Va.

Here's one of the world's true musical wonders. Stalactites covering three acres are connected to and activated by keys on a console organ. When they are struck by electronically controlled rubber-tipped hammers or plungers, this organ produces concert-quality music.

Metropolitan Museum of Art, Instrument Collection, New York, N.Y.

This museum has two fabulous instrument galleries, one for European and one for Asian instruments. These fascinating collections include everything from various musicians' gadgets to musical clocks and boxes. Some of the most unusual instruments are shaped like fish, peacocks, and dragons.

The Musical Museum, Deansboro, N.Y.

This family-run "please touch" museum in upstate New York contains thirteen rooms filled with old-time instruments: nickelodeons, music boxes, and hand-ground organs.

Music City, Nashville, Tenn.

The country music capital has more museums than a guitar has strings. There's the Country Music Hall of Fame, the Music Valley Wax Museum of the Stars, the Hank Williams, Jr., Museum, and the one called Barbara Mandrell Country. Within driving distance there's the House of Cash (Johnny Cash),

Twitty City (Conway Twitty), and Dollywood (Dolly Parton),
in Pigeon Forge.

FIVE MUSICIANS WHO BECAME CITY STATUES

Musician/Accomplishment	City
Louis Armstrong, trumpeter	New Orleans
George M. Cohan, performer/songwriter	New York
Duke Ellington, pianist	New York
Stephen Foster, songwriter	Pittsburgh
Richard Tucker, opera singer	New York

THREE WAYS TO CELEBRATE BIRTHDAYS WITH MUSIC

Touch-Tone Birthday Greeting

The next time a friend has a birthday, call up and tell him or
her to listen, then tap these buttons (you can practice the
rhythm first with the phone off the hook):

```
1 1   4 1   *   9
1 1   4 1   #   0
1 1   # 0   *   7 4
1 1   0 *   0   *
```

Make a Recording

Record a song to play at birthday parties. The Sing-Along
booths in department stores and malls provide you with
everything you need: a list of songs, a private rehearsal and
recording booth, a mike, and a headset through which you
can hear the instruments and voices. Save money by making
your recording with a friend or, if it's a present for your
parents, with a brother or sister.

Create a Personalized Cassette

If you live in a big city, look for a record store that features the Personics system. This setup allows you to create a cassette from a huge catalog of songs and sound effects. Use your imagination to put together a really special birthday gift.

COLLECTING

People are naturally collectors, and music is one of the best fields for putting together interesting collections. Some musical collectibles are priced way beyond kid budgets, but many more are in the "free to affordable" category.

NINE TOP COLLECTIBLES

Item	Collecting Tip
Autographs	For the price of two stamps (one to send your letter, and one to put on a self-addressed, stamped envelope) you can put together a collection of your favorite stars' autographs. Be sure to print or type your request!
Instruments	Visit toy and gift shops for inexpensive toy instruments and instrument-shaped novelty items.
Music Books	Check out library book sales, garage sales, and flea markets for inexpensive, interesting items. The low-cost paperback biographies of new superstars or groups often become valuable collectibles no matter what happens to the stars featured in them.
Music Stamps and Stickers	Available from your local post office, stamp dealers, and gift shops.

Item	*Collecting Tip*
Programs from Music Events	Ask friends and relatives to save their programs for you, and watch your collection grow.
Records	CDs may be what people buy in record stores, but the old 45 r.p.m. records and LP albums are still great collectibles. They can be bought very cheaply at garage sales. Keep your eye out for records from the early days of rock, especially anything by the Beatles and Elvis Presley. An original of "Yesterday" would be a super "rockabilia" find.
Sheet Music	Garage sales often have whole stacks of old song sheets. Some are valuable, and all are great for framing.
Superstar Photos	Like autographs, these are available for the cost of a letter and, in this case, a large stamped, self-addressed envelope.
T-Shirts with Musical Motifs	Wear some, and consider mounting your favorites on a wall board.

Getting in Touch with the Stars

You can write to most recording artists in care of the company they record with. For classical musicians, and some other performers, their agents are the best contacts. Many of the established as well as up-and-coming musicians have fan clubs. These clubs often remain active even after a star no longer shines quite as brightly.

The Record Label Link-up
Acme Music Corp.
259 W. 10 St.
New York, NY 10014

Arista Records (RCA)
6 W. 57 St.
New York, NY 10019

218 Harding Pl.
Nashville, TN 37205

Atco (Atlantic)
   Records
75 Rockefeller Plaza
New York, NY 10019

Agnes Bruneu Associates
Dorchester Towers,
   155 W. 68 St., Ste. 1010
New York, NY 10023
Violinist Joshua Bell.

Capitol Records
34 Music Square East
Nashville, TN 37203

CBS (Epic/Columbia)
34 Music Square East
Nashville, TN 37203

Elektra/Asylum/Nonesuch
   Records
1710 Grand Ave.
Nashville, TN 37212

EMI-United Artists Records
29 Music Square East
Nashville, TN 37203

I.C.M. Artists Ltd.
40 W. 57 St.
New York, NY 10019
Cellist Yo Yo Ma and
   violinist Midori.

MCA Records
70 Universal City Plaza
Universal City, CA 91608

27 Music Square East
Nashville, TN 37203
Bobby Brown.

Motown Record Corp.
6255 Sunset Blvd.
Los Angeles, CA 90028

Geffen Records
9130 Sunset Blvd.
Los Angeles, CA 90069

David Geffen Co.
1755 Broadway
New York, NY 10019

Polygram (Mercury-
   Phonogram/Polydor)
8335 Sunset Blvd.
Los Angeles, CA 90069

810 Seventh Ave.
New York, NY 10019

RCA (A&M Records)
595 Madison Ave.
New York, NY 10022

30 Music Square West
Nashville, TN 37203

Virgin Records
30 W. 21 St.
New York, NY 10010
Paula Abdul.

Warner Brothers
3 E. 54 St.
New York, NY 10022

P.O. Box 120897
Nashville, TN 37212

7250 Beverly Blvd.
Los Angeles, CA 90028

*The Fan Club Connection**

ANA Fan Club
c/o Parc Records
3016 Dade Ave., 2 Floor
Orlando, FL 32804

Backstage with Bon Jovi
P.O. Box 326
Fords, NJ 08863

Debbie Gibson Fan Club
P.O. Box 489
Merrick, NY 11566

Guys Next Door Fan Club
P.O. Box 11100
Aurora, CO 80011

Janet Jackson Fan Club
14755 Ventura Blvd.,
Suite 1-710
Sherman Oaks, CA 91403

Madonna Fan Club
P.O. Box 77505
San Francisco, CA 94107

Richard Marx
2519 Carmen Crest Dr.
Los Angeles, CA 90068

George Michael
George Michael I.F.C.
P.O. Box 302
San Francisco, CA 94101

New Kids on the Block
Official Fan Club
and
Quincy Fan Club
P.O. Box 7001
Quincy, MA 02269

Tommy Page Fan Club
15237 Sunset Blvd.
Pacific Palisades, CA 90272

*Compiled by *SuperTeen* Magazine.

Poison Fan Club
P.O. Box 8668
San Francisco, CA 94101

Tommy Puett Fan Club
2040 Avenue of the Stars
Los Angeles, CA 90068

Sweet Sensation Fan Club
Artists Only
152-18 Union Turnpike,
    Ste. 12S
Flushing, NY 11367

Tiffany
T.I.F.F.
P.O. Box 604
San Francisco, CA 94101

Five Tips for Making Your Album and Singles Collections More Valuable and Enjoyable

• Organize everything so that you can find what you want when you want it.
• Use one of these classification systems: Alphabetical order by the names of the performers and titles, or else by the musical category—classical, rock 'n' roll, country, folk music, or crossover.
• Label everything. Put the labels on the case, not the disc, record, or cassette.
• As your collection grows, make a permanent catalog of it. This can either be a simple list in a notebook or an index card system. If your family owns a computer, you can keep your index in what is called a simple database (a computer term for a collection of facts).
• To make your catalog more interesting and useful, add additional facts for each item you catalog. This could be anything you like, from facts about a song's recording history to information about the recording artists.

RIDDLE 'N' ROCK FUN

People collect and make up riddles because they're fun, funny, and full of surprises. Like folk songs, riddles get passed along from family to family and friend to friend, often with a new twist.

Call and Response

What type of music do you play on Father's day?
Pop rock.

What singer sounds like Michael Jackson, dances like Michael Jackson, and looks like Michael Jackson?
Michael Jackson.

Why do some people think musicians are lazy?
Because all they do is play.

What do ballplayers and musicians have in common?
They both need good scores.

What makes more noise than a heavy metal band?
Two heavy metal bands.

Where will an electric guitar player be when the electricity goes off?
In the dark.

What dance is named after a United States president?
The Polk-a.

What's the difference between Madonna and a bee?
One sings and one stings.

What would happen if you put your stereo inside the refrigerator?
You'd get very cool music.

For Word Watchers

How do you spell music in four letters?
T u n e.

Why is the clarinet a wordy instrument?
Because it spells *act, air, ale, ant, arc, are, can, cant, car,*

care, cat, clan, clean, clear, ear, éclair, ice, inlet, ire, irate, lane, late, let, line, lint, nail, near, net, rain, tail, tale, tan, tear, tile, tin, tine, trail, train.

What instrument looks like an overgrown violin and sounds like a dessert?
The cello.

How do you spell "Yankee Doodle Dandy" in four letters?
S o n g.

How do you spell "The Star-Spangled Banner" in six letters?
A n t h e m.

What instrument do you get when you combine the letter B *with the name of an animal?*
A bass.

Can you name a musical style that's the same spelled forward and backward?
Pop.

Daffynitions

Rubber band. A band that snaps more than it raps.
Rocker. A musical chair.
Hymn. A male religious song.
Snowball. A wintertime dance.

It's all A-rhythm-etic

A band had twenty players. All but three quit. How many were left?
Three.

What kind of musician has six legs?
One who plays sitting on a chair.

What's the difference between a sixteen-year-old rock star and a thirty-year old rock star?
Fourteen years.

How many musicians can you fit onto an empty stage?
None, because then it wouldn't be empty.

A MUSICAL CALENDAR FOR KIDS

CHAPTER 12

This calendar is a catchall of musical firsts, birthdays, and events. You'll find out when the children of Hamelin were lured into the mountains by the Pied Piper and when to send a birthday card to your favorite star. Surprise your friends with some of the wackier musical events, like the marching band with 3,182 musicians that played at the Los Angeles Dodgers stadium in 1985. Record the facts you like best into your own personal diary, along with any new ones that pop up during the year ahead.

KEY TO SYMBOLS

 Birthdays　　 Events　　 Firsts

JANUARY

 1 Paul Revere is best known as an American patriot, but he was also a fine music engraver. He was born on this day in 1735.

 2 Chamber Huang gave the troops in the Saudi desert a chance to create their own music when he sent off a shipment of harmonicas on this day in 1991.

 3 Anna Pavlova, the world-famous ballet dancer, born in 1885.

 4 The Braille system enables the blind to read words and music. It was named after its inventor, Louis Braille, who was himself blind. He was born on this day in 1809.

 5 The first American album, "Where Does My Heart Beat Now?", by French-Canadian pop star Celine Dion, reached no. 1 on the 1991 Hot 100 charts.

 6 In 1963 on this day a musical version of Charles Dickens novel *Oliver Twist* opened on Broadway. One of the kids in the London company was future pop star–songwriter Phil Collins.

7 The first public concert by two musically gifted kids, Wolfgang Amadeus Mozart, age six, and his sister Nannerl, age twelve. The year was 1762. See November 19 for another famous brother-sister team.

JANUARY

 8 On this final day of the War of 1812 the soldiers sang a folk song called "The Eighth of January." In 1955 a schoolteacher named Jimmy Driftwood rewrote it as "The Battle of New Orleans." Four years later it became a no. 1 hit.

 9 Crystal Gayle, who followed in her older sister Loretta Lynn's footsteps as a successful country singer, born 1951.

 10 On this day in 1991 it was announced that jazz would become a regular part of New York City's Lincoln Center of the Performing Arts repertory.

 11 At a Madison Square Garden concert held on this day in 1991, Bell Biv DeVoe introduced their own version of their first group, New Edition. If their producing effort pays off, their teen sextet, ABC, should have rung up a hit or two by the time you read this.

 12 An important new concert hall, named Town Hall, opened in New York on this day in 1921. It still exists.

 13 The first patent for an accordion was issued to Anthony Fass of Philadelphia in 1854.

 14 Albert Schweitzer born 1875. He was best known as a medical missionary, but he was also a professional organist.

JANUARY

 15 The first antiwar music video was released in 1991, a day before the Persian Gulf War's official start. It featured John Lennon's "Give Peace a Chance," with new lyrics by his fifteen-year-old son Sean.

 16 On this day in 1875 Americans heard Johannes Brahms' "Hungarian Dances" played for the first time. Why not borrow the recording from the library?

 17 In 1990 on this date the Rock-and-Roll Hall of Fame celebrated its fifth annual ceremony. Some of the rock legends inducted into it were Hank Ballard, The Platters, Simon and Garfunkel, and The Who.

 18 This was the day to pull down the lavish sets and computerized spotlights of "Rock in Rio II, 1991." This nine-day festival was the most expensive ever. It cost $20 million, including $200,000 for a new lawn in Maracana Stadium.

 19 Country singer Dolly Parton born 1946 in Sevier County, Tennessee.

 20 Composer Joseph Haydn's "Surprise Symphony" was first performed in America on this day in 1881. Go back to Chapter 1 to find out how it got this name.

 21 This is the day in 1903 when "The Wizard of Oz" was first performed as a Broadway musical.

JANUARY

 22 While Paula Abdul was collecting two awards on this day at the 1990 American Music Awards ceremony, thieves helped themselves to $3,400 worth of jewelry from her apartment. Fame does have its drawbacks!

 23 The Rock and Roll Hall of Fame held its first ceremony. The year was 1986. Chuck Berry was the first musician to be inducted into it.

 24 On this day in 1858 Felix Mendelssohn's overture to "A Midsummer Night's Dream" was first used as a wedding march. The bride was Queen Victoria's daughter.

 25 Robert Burns, who wrote the words to "Auld Lang Syne," born 1759.

 26 On this day in 1934 the Apollo Theatre in New York City opened its doors as a showcase for African-American musicians. In 1991 both En Vogue and Sweet Sensation appeared on "Showtime at the Apollo."

 27 Wolfgang Amadeus Mozart, born 1756. As a child performer he was often treated as a freak. People would cover his hands as he played the piano, make him compose tunes on the spot, and perform all sorts of other musical tricks.

28 "Rule, Britannia," Great Britain's most famous patriotic march, was published on this day in 1741.

JANUARY/FEBRUARY

 **29** Dictator Adolf Hitler became head of state in Germany in 1933, and many musicians left this country noted for its great composers.

 30 The Original Dixieland "jass" Band recorded the first-ever jazz recording, "The Darktown Strutters Ball," in 1917.

 31 On this day in 1970 "I Want You Back" became the Jackson Five's first no. 1 hit. It's now a collector's item.

FEBRUARY

 1 To celebrate Black History Month, find out more about some of our great African-American musicians like Count Basie, Duke Ellington, or Ella Fitzgerald. The list of subjects is endless.

 2 Birthday of country music star Clint Black, in 1962.

 3 Twenty-two-year-old Buddy Holly and his entire band died in a plane crash on this day in 1959. His fans refer to this date as "the day the music died." In 1990 his life became the basis for a Broadway musical.

FEBRUARY

4 The U.S.O. (United Service Organizations), which brings entertainment to U.S. troops abroad, celebrated its fiftieth anniversary in 1991. The World War II troops' favorite song, "Boogie Woogie Bugle Boy of Company C," was replaced by "Jump" during the Persian Gulf War, which occurred during the organization's anniversary year.

5 In 1989 Teddy Riley invented a much-imitated dance-pop style known as the *new jack swing*. Its combination of gospel, rap, R&B, and pop-jazz brought success to Teddy and his group, Guy.

6 This was the day in 1991 when the world of soul music lost one of its leaders, Reverend James Cleveland. He taught Aretha Franklin to sing soul and wrote and arranged more than four hundred gospel songs, including "Everything Will Be All Right."

7 Less than two weeks after the Persian Gulf War started in 1991, the first music show especially for the troops was shot at Cher's flag-draped California home. This two-hour videotaped song collection featured Janet Jackson, Paul Simon, Bonnie Raitt, Van Halen, and others.

8 One of Elton John's early hits, "Crocodile Rock," landed on the top of the pop charts on this day in 1973.

9 The British supergroup the Beatles made their first appearance on American television on this day in 1964.

FEBRUARY

 10 Bob Dylan and Bruce Springsteen weren't the first harmonica-playing star performers. Larry Adler, born on this day in 1914, was also a world-renowned performer, one of the few harmonica players to be labeled a genuine virtuoso.

 11 Soul queen Patti LaBelle's first solo hit, "Lady Marmalade," topped the charts on this day in 1975.

 12 The Grammys have become such a big deal that they involve all sorts of pre-award celebrations that bring lots of music lovers to the city where the awards are held. That's why New York City's Mayor David Dinkins declared this day the beginning of Grammy Week in 1991.

13 A musical highlight of *glasnost* in 1990 was when cellist-conductor Mstislav Rostropovich returned to Russia after a sixteen-year absence. Russian listeners cheered wildly when he played one of America's favorite marches, "Stars and Stripes Forever."

 14 "The Blue Danube" waltz was first performed on this day in 1867. If you ever visit Austria you'll discover that the Danube River changes from green to gray to yellow to brown—but it's never blue.

15 Move over, Mariah Carey and Whitney Houston! Celine Dion's title song from her debut album, "Where Does My Heart Beat Now?" made it on this day in 1991 to the Top 10 singles charts, just behind Mariah's "Someday" and a few songs ahead of Whitney's "All the Man I Need."

16 On this day in 1991 the songwriters and directors of the hit musical "Annie" held auditions for "Annie 2." The verdict about this sequel's success should be in by the time you read this.

FEBRUARY

 17 In 1991 on this day disc jockeys all over the country began to report getting lots of requests to play "We Are with You." It was written by a member of the U.S. Navy's country band when the Persian Gulf War began.

 18 "Rock and Roll Waltz," the first hit song with a rock 'n' roll title, went to the top of the 1956 *Billboard* charts.

 19 Thomas Alva Edison registered his patent for the phonograph on this day in 1877.

 20 When the 1990 Grammys were awarded on this day they included two new categories: best alternative music recording, and rap.

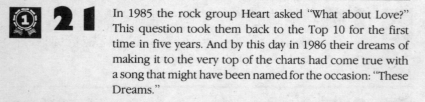 **21** In 1985 the rock group Heart asked "What about Love?" This question took them back to the Top 10 for the first time in five years. And by this day in 1986 their dreams of making it to the very top of the charts had come true with a song that might have been named for the occasion: "These Dreams."

 22 On this day in 1923 Frederick A. Juilliard set up a million-dollar fund to establish a music school. It became one of the world's leading music and dance schools.

 **23** ASCAP was organized on this day in 1913. It has helped songwriters earn money from public performances of their work ever since.

FEBRUARY

 24 Every kid who takes piano lessons eventually plays something by Frédéric Chopin. This Polish composer's first Paris concert took place on this day in 1832.

 25 Enrico Caruso, one of the greatest opera singers of all time, born 1873.

 6 Country singer Johnny Cash, born 1932.

 27 Johann Rellstad, who established the first music-lending library ever, born 1759 in Berlin.

 28 Actor-singer-dancer-musical theater director Tommy Tune, born 1939, in Wichita Falls, Texas.

 9 Opera composer Gioacchino Rossini born 1792. His overtures to *The Barber of Seville* and *William Tell* are often played in movies and on TV. Although Rossini composed lots of music, he was considered lazy. He worked mostly in his bed, and if a sheet of music fell on the floor he'd write a new piece of music so he wouldn't have to bend down to pick it up.

MARCH

 1 In 1990 on this day superstar Janet Jackson kicked off her first-ever live (with a little prerecorded help) tour.

  2 Jon Bon Jovi, the lead singer of the group that bears his name, born 1962.

 3 Paula Abdul's "Forever Your Girl" settled in for its second month at the top of the 1990 charts.

 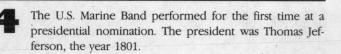 **4** The U.S. Marine Band performed for the first time at a presidential nomination. The president was Thomas Jefferson, the year 1801.

 5 On this day in 1907 Lee De Forest made the first radio broadcast. Celebrate this historic event by listening to the music he played, the William Tell Overture.

  6 Harvard College organized the first college orchestra ever. The year was 1808.

 7 On this day in 1968 Charlie Brown and the gang became Broadway stars. "You're a Good Man, Charlie Brown" played for 1,597 performances and is still a favorite school musical.

MARCH

 8 The *Apollo* astronauts began this day of their 1969 space voyage by singing "Happy Birthday."

 9 Pulitzer Prize–winning American composer Samuel Barber, born 1910.

 10 The Salvation Army established itself in the United States on this day in 1880. Since then Christmas shopping hasn't been the same without this Army's brass bands.

 11 In 1990, composer-producer Quincy Jones's birthday and the Soul Train Music Awards fell on the same day. The occasion was marked with a nationally televised salute.

 12 "Les Miserables," a new musical based on an old book, opened on Broadway on this day in 1987.

 **13** Neil Sedaka, the first rock singer-songwriter-pianist to study at the Juilliard School of Music, born 1939. He made a comeback when he recorded with Elton John.

 **14** Albert Einstein, the mathematician and an enthusiastic amateur violinist, born 1879.

MARCH

 15 The first roller-skating musical, "Starlight Express," rolled onto the Broadway stage on this date in 1987.

 16 Two movies about the exotic dance the lambada were released on this day in 1990, *Lambada* and *The Forbidden Dance*.

 17 To celebrate St. Patrick's Day, learn an Irish clog dance or take out a recording by The Chieftains or Irish pop star Sinead O'Connor.

 18 The female rock group the Go-Gos split up in 1984, but they reunited on this day in 1990 for a concert to benefit the environment.

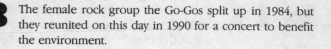 **19** *The Rocky Horror Picture Show* movie about the early days of rock 'n' roll was shown for the first time, in 1975.

 20 When a tractor-trailer crashed into Gloria Estefan's tour bus on this day in 1990, the lead singer of the Miami Sound Machine discovered just how many fans she had. Even President George Bush sent his good wishes.

 21 Johann Sebastian Bach, the most famous member of a large musical family, born 1685.

MARCH

 2 Attention, stamp collectors: On this day in 1990 the U.S. Postal Service issued a stamp to honor the movie *The Wizard of Oz*.

 3 "We Are the World," the charity record that featured over forty major musicians, became the top-selling record on the charts on this day in 1985.

 4 A group called the Quarrymen Skiffle made its first public appearance on this day in 1962. They later renamed themselves the Beatles.

 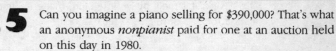 **5** Can you imagine a piano selling for $390,000? That's what an anonymous *nonpianist* paid for one at an auction held on this day in 1980.

 6 Since this is Make Up a Holiday Day, why not invent your own special music celebration?

 7 Singer and jazz legend Sarah Vaughan, born 1924. She was nicknamed the divine Sarah.

  8 This is the day in 1788 when Maryland became the seventh state of the United States. Can you hum its official song, "Maryland, My Maryland"?

MARCH/APRIL

 29 The Royal Albert Hall in London first opened its doors on this day in 1871. From January 18 to February 10, 1990, it became Eric Hall, in honor of rock guitarist Eric Clapton's annual concerts at the still-famous hall.

 30 Former Led Zeppelin front man Robert Plant's fans got a chance to listen to his newly released 1990 album, "Manic Nirvana."

 31 Joseph Haydn, the composer often credited with being the father of the symphony, born 1732.

APRIL

 1 "Nick of Time," by Bonnie Raitt, made its first appearance at the top of the 1990 hit parade.

 2 Attention, collectors: On this day in 1990 a postcard to honor Carnegie Hall was issued.
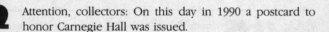

 3 If you're a fan of 1990's new group called Homework, you might want to send birthday greetings to Shawn Meadows, born 1973.

 4 Blues singer-guitarist-composer Muddy Waters was born in 1915 on this date. He influenced many of today's rock 'n' roll musicians. Check the section on "The Stories Behind Eight Famous Stage Names" in Chapter 2 to find out which famous group named itself after one of his songs.

APRIL

 5 Some people considered Spanish singer Julio Iglesias and country star Willie Nelson an unlikely combination. But enough bought their recording of "To All the Girls I've Loved Before" for it to become a *Billboard* best seller on this day in 1984.

 6 On this day in 1917, immediately after the United States had entered World War I, George M. Cohan wrote that war's chief marching song: "Over There."

 7 This was the 1949 opening day of the Pulitzer Prize–winning musical "South Pacific."

  8 Julian Lennon, son of ex-Beatle John Lennon and himself a rock star, born 1963.

 9 By this date in 1991, "Kiss You All Over," by "Life Goes On" star Tommy Puett, had begun to heat up the airwaves. Devyn Page, Tommy's kid sister of Kids, Inc., was the backup singer.

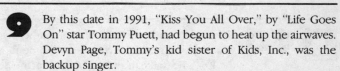 **10** On this day in 1979 record sales were first classified according to their type of music. Rock music accounted for 41.7 percent of all the categories in this first listing.

 11 The old-fashioned barbershop quartets may be finished, but not for lack of trying by O. C. Cash. In 1938 he founded the SPEBSQS (The Society for the Preservation of Barbershop-Quartet Singing) on this day.

APRIL

 12 Barn-dance programs were the first country-music radio shows. The first such program aired on this day in 1924.

 13 A New York newspaper reported that Ben Franklin had invented an instrument he called the 'armonica. The year was 1762.

 14 Loretta Lynn, the country singer whose autobiography became the basis for the movie *Coalminer's Daughter*, born 1935 in Butcher's Hollow, Kentucky.

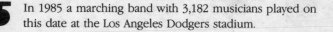 **15** In 1985 a marching band with 3,182 musicians played on this date at the Los Angeles Dodgers stadium.

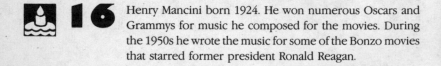 **16** Henry Mancini born 1924. He won numerous Oscars and Grammys for music he composed for the movies. During the 1950s he wrote the music for some of the Bonzo movies that starred former president Ronald Reagan.

17 In 1912 newspapers throughout the world were filled with stories of the tragic sinking of the *Titanic* two days earlier. One of the most moving stories described the ship's musicians, who tried to maintain calm by bravely continuing to play.

 18 Fiorello La Guardia was one of New York City's most musical mayors. On this day in 1941 he conducted a benefit concert at Carnegie Hall for the firemen.

APRIL

 19 Singer Smokey Robinson, whose hit-making group the Miracles put Motown records on the musical map, was born on this day in 1940. He was inducted into the Rock and Roll Hall of Fame in 1987.

 20 Grammy Award–winner Luther Vandross born 1959.

 21 A date for musical traffic jams: in 1749, carriages headed for the first public rehearsal of Handel's "Fireworks Music" stopped traffic over London Bridge for three hours. The musical celebrations for the twentieth anniversary of Earth Day caused major traffic jams 250 years later.

 22 Glenn Campbell, who brought a pop sound to country music, born 1936.

 23 Audiences at London's Haymarket Theatre on this day in 1746 heard a most unusual concert. It featured twenty-six drinking glasses tuned with spring water that were accompanied by a band.

24 In 1989 Massachusetts Governor Michael Dukakis declared this to be New Kids on the Block Day, in honor of this group's antidrug efforts.

 25 Audiences who attended the New Theater in Philadelphia on this day in 1798 heard the words to "Hail, Columbia" for the first time. They already knew the tune as "The President's March."

APRIL/MAY

 26 On this day in 1861 the old German folk song "Oh, Tannenbaum" began a new life as "Maryland, My Maryland."

 27 Ma Rainey, the legendary country blues singer, born 1886.

 28 Sinead O'Connor's "I Do Not Want What I Haven't Got" bumped Bonnie Raitt's "Nick of Time" off the top spot on the 1990 charts.

 29 Edward "Duke" Ellington, the American jazz pianist and composer, born 1899.

 30 Charles Cros deposited his idea for a phonograph with the French Academy of Sciences on this day in 1876. However, the patent for the invention went to Thomas Edison in America.

MAY

 1 It's Mother Goose Day. If you haven't looked through the trivia questions and answers in Chapter 9 yet, look up the name of the nursery rhyme that was jazzed up into a chart-topping hit. See if you can sing a nursery rhyme song in a jazzy modern beat.

 2 Kids of all ages love "Peter and the Wolf," which was first heard on this day in Moscow in 1939.

MAY

Most musicals come and go, but not "The Fantasticks." It opened on this day in 1960—and it's still playing!

 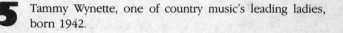

This was the day in 1958 when the first Grammy Awards ceremony was held.

Tammy Wynette, one of country music's leading ladies, born 1942.

La Boheme, an opera full of hummable arias (that's opera talk for songs), had its world premiere in Venice in 1896.

Take out a recording by one or both of these two great composers who were born this day: Johannes Brahms (1833) and Peter Ilyich Tchaikovsky (1840).

"Home Sweet Home" was heard for the first time on this day in 1823. It was in an opera entitled *Clari, The Maid of Milan*.

Attention, Billy Joel fans: He was born on this day in 1949, in Levittown, Long Island.

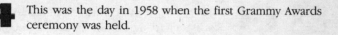

MAY

 10 Can you imagine marching and playing for 37.9 miles? A Norwegian marching band did just that, on this day in 1990. It's the longest musical march on record.

 11 In 1990 ASCAP and Carnegie Hall teamed up to celebrate songwriter Irving Berlin's hundredth birthday. Watch for rebroadcasts of this Emmy Award–winning event.

 12 Jeanette Gloria La Bianca, who had appeared in two major operas before she even turned sixteen, born 1934.

 13 Superstar Steveland Morris (Stevie Wonder), born 1950.

 14 Donnie Wood (Daniel William, Jr.) of New Kids on the Block fame, born 1970.

 **15** Next time you hum a tune from *The Wizard of Oz*, remember the author of the book: L. Frank Baum, born 1856.

16 Janet Jackson, born 1966.

MAY

 17 Jordan Knight was born on this date in 1971. What do you think he and the other New Kids on the Block will be doing by 1995?

 18 The first issue of the first music magazine in America, *Musical America*, was published on this day in 1876.

 19 Sinead O'Connor's "I Do Not Want What I Haven't Got" completed a full month at the top of the 1990 charts. And it wasn't the last one!

20 On this date in 1979 the National Academy of Recording Arts and Sciences created a special rock Grammy Award. Before this, rock had been part of a general pop music category.

21 Old musicals, like old records, frequently enjoy comeback successes, as did "Gypsy." It opened to rave reviews on this date in 1959. Thirty years later it made a big comeback, with TV star Tyne Daly.

 22 Opera composer Richard Wagner was born on this day in 1813. Thousands of Wagnerians (superenthusiastic fans) continue to flock to his marathon-length musical dramas. Many movies and cartoon shows have used his music as background.

 23 Several years ago Michigan's governor proclaimed this to be Aretha Franklin Day.

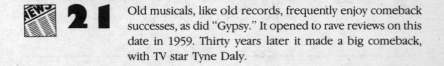

MAY

 24 Second-generation country singer Roseanne Cash (Johnny Cash is her dad), born 1955.

 25 Madonna's album "I'm Breathless," from the movie *Dick Tracy*, was first released on this day in 1990. It included three songs by one of Broadway's top composers, Stephen Sondheim.

 26 An oldtimer and an upcoming star share this birthday: Al Jolson, the first performer to sing in a sound movie (*The Jazz Singer*), born 1866, and David Knight (member of Homework) in 1968.

 27 Julia Ward Howe, who wrote the lyrics for "The Battle Hymn of the Republic," born 1819. In 1991, a brand-new arrangement was recorded by her great-great-great-granddaughter, Jennifer Everett Putnam.

 28 On this date in 1935 the jazz magazine *Down Beat* used the word *swing* for the first time. In 1990 swing dancing made a big comeback, especially with college students.

 29 This was the day in 1942 when actor-singer Bing Crosby recorded "White Christmas." It's been breaking sales records around the world ever since.

30 Not satisfied with the Exxon Corporation's efforts to clean up Alaska's waters after the 1990 *Valdez* oil spill, the group Midnight Oil gave a lunch-time protest concert. The banner on their outdoor stage read "Midnight Oil Makes You Dance . . . Exxon Oil Makes Us Sick."

MAY/JUNE

 31 Peter Yarrow was born on this day in 1938. He was a member of Peter, Paul, and Mary, one of the major folk rock groups from the 1960s who still perform together occasionally.

JUNE

 1 Mariah Carey began her 1990 ride to pop rock stardom.

 2 Tiffany, the youngest-ever pop singer with a no. 1 album, was the first to rise to the top by singing at shopping malls, born 1971.

 3 To buy a Stradivarius violin you're more likely to go to an auction house than a music store. On this day in 1971 virtuoso Yehudi Menuhin performed on a 250-year-old Stradivarius at Sotheby's auction house. It then sold for $200,000.

 4 Freddy Fender, who helped to popularize a type of country music called Tex-Mex, born Baldemar G. Huerta in 1937.

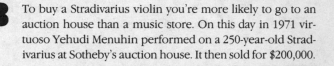 **5** The International Spoleto Festival, now an annual event, began on this date in 1958.

 6 The Black Music Association was formed in 1978 on this day to help its members improve their incomes as musicians. And on this date a year later President Jimmy Carter gave a dinner reception to further their cause.

JUNE

  7 Graceland, Elvis Presley's Tennessee home, opened its doors to tourists on this day in 1982.

 8 The post office issued another in its series of Stamps for the Performing Arts. The 1990 release honored composer Cole Porter.

 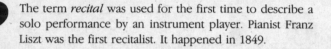 **9** The term *recital* was used for the first time to describe a solo performance by an instrument player. Pianist Franz Liszt was the first recitalist. It happened in 1849.

 10 Judy Garland, known to most kids as Dorothy in *The Wizard of Oz*, born 1922. The name on her birth certificate reads Frances Ethel Gumm.

 11 On this day in 1949 a sad-looking young man named Hank Williams made his debut at the Grand Ole Opry. He became a country music legend. His son, Hank Williams, Jr., carries on the family singing tradition.

 12 Chick Corea, the Grammy Award–winning electronic keyboard musician, born 1941.

 13 Terence Trent D'Arby's second of three 1988 Top 40 hits, "Sign Your Name," started its fifteen-week run today. Look in Chapter 2 to find out why he might be called a two-fisted player.

JUNE

 14 Gloria Estefan and the Miami Sound Machine sounded off with a big hit song, "Anything for You," on this date in 1988.

 15 M. C. Hammer's 1990 tour got off the ground in true superstar style. His fifteen dancers, dozens of background singers, eight security guards, seven musicians, and two DJs flew off in his private jet.

 **16** Today is Song Power Day, a reminder that songs have the power to unite and bring joy to people.

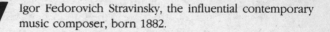 **17** Igor Fedorovich Stravinsky, the influential contemporary music composer, born 1882.

 18 Today "Together Forever" rocked singer Rick Astley all the way to first place on the 1988 charts.

 19 Lisa Lisa and Cult Jam have had many pop dance hits, including "Head to Toe," which danced all the way up the charts on this day in 1987.

 **20** The first television broadcast of an operetta, "The Pirates of Penzance," happened in 1939.

JUNE

 21 Recorded music took another step forward on this day in 1948 when Dr. Peter Goldmark of CBS demonstrated the first long playing (LP) record.

 22 Adolphe Sax invented the saxophone in 1840. But he didn't take out a patent on it until this day in 1846.

 23 In 1990, thirty years after Buddy Holly last played his Fender Stratocaster electric guitar, Sotheby's auction house sold it for $250,000. The buyer? The actor who played Buddy in the movie *The Buddy Holly Story*.

 24 On or about this date each year, musical kids from all over the country come to the Interlochen Music Camp in northern Michigan. You'll find the address in Chapter 11.

 25 London-born superstar George Michael, born 1963.

 26 When Antonia Brico was born on this day in 1902, there were few opportunities for women conductors. In 1935 she created her own opportunity by organizing a Women's Symphony Orchestra.

 27 Bell Laboratory technicians demonstrated the first color TV sets on this day in 1929. It took many more years for color television to make its way into most homes.

JUNE/JULY

28 Richard Rodgers, the famous composer for the musical stage, born 1902. In 1990 a Broadway theater was named in his honor.

29 This was the last day of South African leader Nelson Mandela's historic 1990 visit to the United States. A farewell concert featured Stevie Wonder, Paula Abdul, Bonnie Raitt, and many other stars.

30 "Step-by-Step" zoomed to the top of the 1990 charts, but for just one week. This started rumblings about a beginning of the end of the New Kids on the Block boom.

JULY

1 On this day in 1862 General David Butterfield wrote "Taps" on the back of an envelope. He wanted a bugle wake-up call to replace the gunshot alarm then in use. He figured that the bugle would wake up only his troops and not be heard by the enemy.

2 In 1896 on this day composer Theodore Metz copyrighted a song closely associated with the Spanish-American War, "A Hot Time in the Old Town."

3 American composer Ruth Crawford Seeger born 1901. Many of the folk songs you enjoy are known because she collected and wrote them down.

4 Stephen Foster, who wrote some 175 songs, born 1826.

JULY

 5 How's this for audience enthusiasm—one and a half hours of applause and eighty-three curtain calls. It happened in 1983 after opera singer Placido Domingo's appearance in *La Boheme* at the state Opera House in Vienna, Austria.

 6 In 1990 the fiftieth anniversary of the Tanglewood Music Festival, in the Berkshire Mountains, was held on this date. Go back to Chapter 11 for details about this annual series of events.

 7 A radio disc jockey played a young Memphis truckdriver's first record. The singer's name: Elvis Presley. The song: "That's All Right." The year: 1954. The rest is rock history!

 8 "Please Hammer Don't Hurt 'Em" settled at the top of the 1990 charts for the second month.

 9 On this date in 1955 "Rock Around the Clock" became the first no. 1 rock 'n' roll record.

 10 Bobbie Leslie and Damon Sharp are two of the Guys Next Door whose popular Saturday morning TV show helped them become a 1990s pop group. Their birthdays are just a day apart: Damon's on this day in 1972, and Bobbie's a day and a year earlier.

 11 The 1990 movie that inspired Billy Idol's hit single "Cradle of Love" was released.

JULY

 12 Richard Stoltzman, the clarinet soloist, born 1942.

 13 This is the anniversary of the Live-Aid concert, the super-successful 1985 fundraising effort that inspired many other such good-cause events.

 14 Woody Guthrie, an American folksinger who composed over 1,000 songs, born 1912.

  15 On this day in 1989 Prince's album of the music from the movie *Batman* topped the charts for the first time.

 16 Grammy Award–winning singer-songwriter Tracy Chapman's career went into high gear on this date in 1988. That's when her record "Fast Car" began a twelve-week ride as a chart buster.

 17 The Newport Jazz Festival, a well-attended annual music event, was organized on this day in 1954.

 18 The first patriotic American tune, "The Liberty Song," was published on this day in 1768.

JULY

 19 If you'd been around on this day in 1911 you could have heard the world's shortest orchestra composition. It lasted all of nineteen seconds!

 20 On this date in 1940 *Billboard* Magazine published its first Musical Popularity Chart. The top-rated record was "I'll Never Smile Again," by Frank Sinatra.

 21 On this day in 1990 the destruction of the wall separating East from West Berlin was celebrated with a performance of Roger Waters' "The Wall." It featured a "cast" of characters inflated to 80-foot heights.

 22 This is the day, in 1376, when legend says the Pied Piper of Hamelin lured all the town's children into a hole in a hill. They were never seen again.

 23 In 1988 this date marked pop star Richard Marx's first leap to the top of the charts, with "Hold On to the Nights."

 24 In 1849 on this day Georgetown University in Washington, D.C., became the first college to offer a doctor of music degree.

 **25** Roseanne Barr entered the Star-Spangled Hall of Shame on this day in 1990 with her screechy performance of the national anthem at a San Diego Padres game. See Chapter 9 for other such anthem-at-the-baseball-game disasters.

JULY

 6 Wolfgang Amadeus Franz Xavier Mozart, born 1791. Compared to his father, Wolfgang Amadeus, he was a slow starter. He didn't give his first concert until he was thirteen. He never did achieve his father's fame.

 27 Up With People is a traveling musical troupe that has been bringing a message of peace, freedom, and togetherness to every state and sixty-nine countries since 1965. On this day in 1990 nearly five thousand former members gathered for a twenty-fifth anniversary celebration.

 28 Western Union introduced the first singing telegram on this day in 1933. Their singing messengers are now long gone, but you could still deliver your own song greeting to Mom and Dad or your best friend.

 9 Charlie Christian, the first musician to use the electric guitar as a jazz instrument, born 1919.

 30 Paul Anka, one of our earliest teen singer-songwriters, born 1941. He wrote his first hit song when he was fifteen. His music was the lead-in theme for the Johnny Carson show.

31 A 1990 lawsuit charged the heavy-metal group Judas Priest with putting hidden messages about suicide into their lyrics. On this day in court, lead singer Ron Halford testified that he once did record a phrase backward, but he said no to the accusation. Tseirp Saduj! The group was found not guilty.

AUGUST

 1 This day sees another anniversary: the rock video cable channel MTV has been around since 1981.

 2 The largest chorus in history was organized on this date in 1937. Sixty thousand singers joined in for the final song at a German choral contest.

  3 La Scala, one of the world's great opera houses, opened on this day in 1778. It remains one of the top sights in Milan, Italy.

  4 This is the day in 1958 when *Billboard* introduced a new scorekeeping category labeled The Hot 100.

 5 Today "American Bandstand" telecast its first show, in 1957. Kids who tuned in heard a song called "I'm Gonna Sit Right Down and Write Myself a Letter."

 6 Every band is out there looking for a big hit. The Irish rock band U2 found theirs with "I Still Haven't Found What I'm Looking For," which reached no. 1 on this day in 1988.

  7 In 1988 on this day Steve Winwood's "Roll With It" rolled into its second week of four at the top of all the top songs.

AUGUST

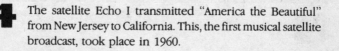

  8

"Please Hammer Don't Hurt 'Em" begins an amazing fourth month at the top of the 1990 charts. For sure, it didn't hurt M. C. Hammer's career!

 9

Whitney Houston, born 1963.

 10

Columbia Pictures released *Postcards from the Edge*, the 1990 movie in which actress Meryl Streep proved her talents as a country singer.

 11

If Eddie Garcia is your favorite in the Guys Next Door, make a note to send him a birthday card today.

 12

Katharine Lee Bates, the author of "America the Beautiful," born 1859.

 13

Sir George Grove, the original editor of the largest and most complete dictionary of music, born 1820.

14

The satellite Echo I transmitted "America the Beautiful" from New Jersey to California. This, the first musical satellite broadcast, took place in 1960.

AUGUST

15 This was the first day of the most written-about musical event of 1969, Woodstock, named after the small New York town where it occurred. More than twenty-four bands played for over 400,000 people. In 1989 many groups who had been there had a twentieth-anniversary celebration.

16 Elvis Presley died on this day in 1977, but his legend lives on.

17 Donnie Wahlberg (Donald, Jr.), the second kid to become a New Kid on the Block, born 1970.

18 On this day in 1990 the Rolling Stones played Prague. This was a wish come true for Mick Jagger fan President Vaclav Havel of Czechoslovakia.

19 In 1988 one of Madonna's biggest hits, "Papa Don't Preach," was in its first of two weeks as the no. 1 song in the land.

20 The "1812 Overture," an American Fourth of July favorite, was first performed on this day in 1882, in Moscow.

21 In 1990 on this day a 7-Eleven store in Tillicum, Wash., discovered that the easiest way to prevent teens from using the store as a hangout was to play "easy listening" music.

AUGUST

 2 Claude Debussy, the French composer, was born on this day in 1862.

 3 In 1990 on this day the original cast of "The Sound of Music" celebrated the twenty-fifth anniversary date of the movie's premiere. Several of the Von Trapp children and cast members who were there now had kids of their own.

 24 In 1990 on this date John Cougar Mellencamp went on location to star in a movie called *Souvenirs*, about a country singer.

  5 Conductor-composer Leonard Bernstein, born 1918.

 6 Lee De Forest, an important inventor in the recorded music field, born in 1873 in Council Bluffs, Iowa.

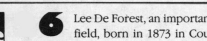 **27** On this day in 1990 blues guitarist Stevie Ray Vaughan died in a plane crash. This tragedy was a sad reminder of the crash that killed the 1960s rock group the Crickets.

  28 On this day in 1838 a South Boston school board hired the first public-school music instructor in America. His name was Lowell Mason.

AUGUST/SEPTEMBER

 29 Birthday greetings to singer-dancer Michael Jackson, born 1958. And Melvin "Finese" Sutton, of Homework, born 1968.

 30 In 1990 the cute Pillsbury doughboy and Campbell Soup kids made their first commercial appearances as rappers.

 31 Debbie Gibson (Deborah Ames), the singer-songwriter who has been a superstar since age sixteen, born 1970.

SEPTEMBER

1 When Oscar Hammerstein II died, the musical theater lost an outstanding composer. To honor the man and his music, every New York theater turned off its lights on this night in 1960.

2 Attention, would-be songwriters looking for subjects: There hasn't been a song about the month of September or autumn for quite a while. "Autumn Leaves" was a big hit, but that was in the 1960s. And Earth, Wind and Fire did score briefly, with "September," but that came in 1975.

3 On this day in 1955 "The Yellow Rose of Texas" went to the top spot on the *Billboard* charts. This rewrite of an 1853 marching song proves that a good song can have more than one life.

4 If you're a fan of Dio Aviles of Homework, wish him a happy birthday. He was born in 1967.

SEPTEMBER

 5 Johann Christian Bach, one of Johann Sebastian Bach's several musical sons, was born on this day in Germany in 1734. After he moved to London he became known as the London Bach.

 6 Another chart-topping week for the awesome "Hammer, Please Don't Hurt 'Em." That's rapping all the way to the bank!

 7 How about one of those make-your-own-song cassettes for grandfather on Granddad's Day?

 8 Bohemian composer Antonin Dvorak was born this day in 1860. When he visited the United States he encouraged American composers to use their native music.

 9 This was the day, in 1846, when Richard Wagner began to work on his opera *Lohengrin*. It remains an opera hit, even though "Here Comes the Bride," based on the "Wedding March" from the opera has fallen on hard times.

 10 Sheena Easton, the singer-actress, born in Glasgow, Scotland, 1959.

 11 On this day in 1959 a statue to honor songwriter George M. Cohan was unveiled in New York City's Duffy Square. Ten thousand people watched and sang his "Give My Regards to Broadway." Today crowds gather near the statue daily to buy half-priced theater tickets.

SEPTEMBER

 12 The first musical ever, "The Black Crook," opened on this day in 1866. The five-and-a-half-hour-long extravaganza ran for over a year.

 13 Bill Monroe, the country music entertainer who discovered and promoted bluegrass music, born 1911 in Kentucky, the bluegrass state.

 14 Francis Scott Key wrote the words to "The Star-Spangled Banner" on this day in 1814.

 15 Bobby McFerrin's "Don't Worry, Be Happy" continued to ride high on the 1988 charts.

 16 Evan Stent, of Homework, born 1967.

 17 Australian singer-actress Kylie Minogue's remake of "The LocoMotion" returned to the popularity charts on this day in 1988—fourteen years after it was a no. 1 hit for a group called Grand Funk Railroad.

 18 The Honolulu Ad Club registered a patent for the ukulele, in 1917.

SEPTEMBER

 19 Michael Jackson and Paul McCartney recorded two no. 1 hits together. The first of these, "The Girl Is Mine," appeared in the top spot on this day in 1988. And here's a coincidence: Jackson's third no. 1 hit for 1970 also reached the top spot on this day.

 20 Jelly Roll Morton, the influential 1920s jazz piano player, born 1885.

 21 Francis Hopkinson, a signer of the Declaration of Independence and the first native-born American composer, born 1737.

 22 Today is Pen Pal Day. Why not write a fan letter?

 **23** John Lomax, the American folk-song collector and founder of the American Folklore Society at the Library of Congress, born 1870.

 24 Jim Henson, the creator of that favorite cartoon vocalist Kermit the Frog, born 1936.

 25 Dmitri Shostakovich, a composer whose music was once condemned as being "un-Soviet," born in 1906.

SEPTEMBER/OCTOBER

 26 Today Emile Berliner patented a disk recording device that made it possible to mass produce phonograph records. The year was 1887.

 27 Michaelangelo, Donatello, Leonardo, and Raphael—better known as the Teen-Age Mutant Ninja Turtles—opened on this day in 1990 in a musical, "Coming Out of Their Shells." Since all their songs were prerecorded, you might say the turtles were the first mask-syncing group ever.

 28 The first patent to print songbooks was issued on this day in 1598 to Thomas Morley, a composer of madrigal songs.

 29 On this day in 1958 "It's All in the Game" hit the top of the *Billboard* charts. This rock version of "Melody in A Major" was based on the one composed by Charles Gates Dawes before he became President Calvin Coolidge's second in command.

 30 On this day in 1977 President Jimmy Carter designated October as the official country music month.

OCTOBER

 1 Julie Andrews, the singing star of *Mary Poppins* and *The Sound of Music*, born 1935.

2 Play some of Charlie Brown and Snoopy's songs today to celebrate the gang's birthday in 1950. Yes, they *are* middle-aged!

OCTOBER

  Chubby Checker, born Ernest Evans in 1941. In 1988 he rerecorded his 1960s hit dance number, "The Twist," with the Fat Boys. It didn't make no. 1, but it did stay in the Top 40 for eight weeks.

 4 On this day in 1988 rock singer-songwriter-producer John Mellencamp began recording as John Cougar Mellencamp.

  5 A piano-playing president, Chester A. Arthur, born 1830. Can you name any other presidents who played the piano? If not, take a look at Chapter 4.

 6 Moviegoers saw their first musical on this day in 1927. It was called "The Jazz Singer."

 7 "Cats," another musical hit by Andrew Lloyd Webber, began a long Broadway run on this day in 1982. It's top cat tune is "Memory."

8 On this day in 1965 "Yesterday," one of the super hits of all time, made its first appearance as no. 1 on the *Billboard* Top 5.

 9 In 1976 Ludwig van Beethoven's "Symphony no. 5 in C Minor" landed for a twenty-two-week stop in the first spot of the Top 5. Beethoven is dead, and this isn't a ghost story. It's simply a case of Beethoven being updated with a disco rock beat and a catchy new title: "A Fifth of Beethoven."

OCTOBER

 10 This is a double celebration for Giuseppe Verdi of his birthday (in 1813) and the first production of his opera *Aida* by an all African-American cast (in 1942).

 11 Jerome Robbins, the Broadway musical choreographer and director, born 1918.

 12 Ralph Vaughan Williams, a British composer whose music often contained his country's folk music, born 1872.

 13 "Red Red Wine" became a red-hot hit for UB40 on this day in 1988. Their group has one of the wackiest origins around. Check it out in Chapter 2 under "Rock Group Nametags."

 14 This was the day in 1972 when "Ben," by Michael Jackson, became the first no. 1 hit ever about a rat.

 15 The first city-owned opera house, the War Memorial Opera House of San Francisco, opened on this day in 1932.

 16 On this day in 1893 a song called "Goodmorning to All" was copyrighted by two teachers who wrote it for their kindergarten pupils. The title was later changed to "Happy Birthday."

OCTOBER

 17 A controversial rock musical, "Hair," opened on this day in 1967. It ran for 1,742 performances and then became a movie.

 18 Wynton Marsalis, one of the best-known modern jazz musicians, born 1962.

 19 The movie version of *Babes in Toyland*, the first musical about teenagers, opened at New York's Capitol Theatre on this date in 1939. Learn one of its songs, "My Funny Valentine," for next February fourteenth.

 20 Charles Ives, the American musician, was born on this day in 1874.

 21 "Dr. Feelgood," by Motley Crue, began its second week as no. 1 on the 1989 charts.

 22 Madonna and other rockers launched a campaign to get people to vote in the November 1990 elections.

 23 In 1878 on this day the opera *Carmen* had its first American performance but was sung in Italian. It took another fifteen years before audiences could hear it in French, the language in which it was written.

OCTOBER

 24 "Brother, Can You Spare a Dime?" was the theme song for the tough economic conditions of the 1930s. It all began when the stock market crashed on this day in 1929. Ten cents went a lot farther then than it does now.

 25 The international violin star Midori, born 1971.

 26 Learn the song written about the Erie Canal, which opened on this day in 1825.

 27 Nicolo Paganini, a superstar violinist, born in Genoa, Italy, in 1782.

 28 In 1813 on this day Franz Schubert, age twelve, finished his first symphony, the "Symphony in D." It's not too early for you to try your hand at writing a song!

 29 In 1990 on this day "Ice Ice Baby," by Vanilla Ice, became the first rap number to top the pop single charts.

 30 The Martha Graham dance company performed a famous contemporary composition called "Appalachian Spring." This debut performance was staged at the Library of Congress, in 1944.

OCTOBER/NOVEMBER

 31 Starting on this day in 1987, George Michael hit a lucky streak. Four of his songs in a row landed on the Top 40. Each stayed there for at least twelve weeks.

NOVEMBER

 1 Frédéric Chopin's famous Polish mazurkas and polonaises may have been inspired by the cup of Polish soil presented to him on this day in 1830 when he left Warsaw for Paris, never to return.

2 On this date in 1989 the Rolling Stones donated $500,000 from their Steel Wheels reunion tour to help the victims of the San Francisco earthquake and Hurricane Hugo.

 3 This was a record-breaking day in 1956. Elvis Presley's "Love Me Tender" moved into the no. 1 position and his "Don't Be Cruel" and "Hounddog" went to no. 2—the first time a performer had ever followed himself into the top spot.

4 The Beach Boys, who combined rock with a calypso beat to give their songs the mood of surfboarding, created a big splash in the 1960s. During this week in 1988 their name once again made the top of the charts with "Kokomo."

 5 Paul Simon, born 1942. His Grammy-winning album "Graceland" led the way toward combining the sounds of rock 'n' roll with music from all parts of the world. In 1990 he did it again with "The Rhythm of the Saints."

 6 Ignace Jan Paderewski, the Polish pianist, composer, and statesman, born 1860.

NOVEMBER

  7 On this day in 1947 *Billboard* started a Top 15 rating chart.

  8 An old favorite, *The Rocky Horror Picture Show*, became an instant best renter on this date in 1990, when it was released as a video.

  9 The first issue of *Rolling Stone* Magazine was published on this day in 1969, with John Lennon on its cover.

 10 Martin Luther, born 1483. He led the Protestant Reformation and composed many hymns.

 11 Dick Clark, the host of the long-lasting "American Bandstand" show, born 1929.

 12 Kate Smith sang "God Bless America" for the first time, on this Armistice Day in 1938. Actually, the song was then twenty years old, but it had never been publicly performed before.

 13 Composer Gioacchino Rossini was very superstitious. He particularly feared Friday the thirteenth. And here's an incredible fact: he died on Friday the thirteenth, in 1868!

NOVEMBER

 4 The Monkees were the Guys Next Door of the 1960s. On this day in 1968 they followed up their first no. 1 hit, "I'm a Believer," with their last, "Daydream Believer."

 15 NBC broadcast its first music program on this day in 1926. It featured the New York Symphony Orchestra and many distinguished soloists.

 16 W. C. (William Christopher) Handy, the famous blues musician, born 1873.

 7 "Tom Dooley," a century-old tune from the Blue Ridge Mountains, hit no. 1 on the *Billboard* Top 5 on this day in 1958. This marked the beginning of a folk music revival.

 18 Sir William Schwenck Gilbert, the lyric-writing half of the team of Gilbert and Sullivan, born 1836.

 19 Composer Felix Mendelssohn and his sister Fanny performed his overture to "A Midsummer Night's Dream" for the first time on this day in 1826. See January seventh for another famous brother-sister prodigy performing team.

 20 This is the day in 1990 when Milli Vanilli became the first-ever musicians to be stripped of their Grammy Awards because of being all sync and no song.

NOVEMBER

 21 Instrument lovers have paid some pretty awesome prices for violins made by Antonio Stradivari. But a red Strad owned by the family of composer Felix Mendelssohn sold on this day in 1990 for an all-time high of $1,700,000.

 22 The Australian rock group Inxs made it to the top of the charts on this day in 1987 with "I Need You Tonight." When you talk about them, say "in excess."

 23 "Fiorello," the first musical about a mayor (Fiorello La Guardia, of New York), opened on Broadway on this day in 1959. It was also the first musical for songwriters Jerry Bock and Sheldon Harnick.

 24 Scott Joplin, one of the greats of ragtime piano, born 1868.

 25 If you'd been a kid on this day in 1947 you would have read about an exciting new recording device developed by J. Bardeen, W. Brattain, and W. Shockley. Their transistor has evolved into today's "Walkman."

26 On this day in 1988 the Barbusters' "Light of Day," the title song of a movie with Michael J. Fox began its second week on the Top 40 list. The band was the fictional band led in the movie by Joan Jett, whom you may know as the leader of the Blackhearts.

27 Around this date each year musicians get into the Christmas spirit with standard and jazzed-up versions of songs ranging from "Silent Night" to "Winter Wonderland" to novelty songs like "Bummed Out Christmas."

NOVEMBER/DECEMBER

 28 The first radio broadcast of the Grand Ole Opry, in 1925.

 29 Jon Knight (Jonathan Rasleigh), one of the New Kids on the Block, born 1969.

 30 In 1977 the 1940s singer-actor Bing Crosby and the English rock star David Bowie sang a duet of "The Little Drummer Boy" on TV. This event was preserved as a video called "Bing Crosby's Merrie Olde Christmas."

DECEMBER

 1 International AIDS Day 1990 inspired a benefit album called "Red, Hot and Blue" on which the biggest and best rock musicians sang songs by composer-lyricist Cole Porter.

 2 Matt Haimovitz, a cellist who began performing in public at age seven and made several dazzling debut performances at sixteen, born 1972 in Israel.

 3 "The Voice of Firestone," one of the best and most popular music programs in the history of radio, began a twenty-year run on this day in 1928. The show also had a successful television life.

4 The tragedy of rock legend Buddy Holly's early death inspired a song that became a no. 1 hit on this day in 1971: "American Pie," recorded by Don McLean.

DECEMBER

 5 Walt Disney, the man behind many much-loved animated musicals, born 1901.

 6 Today is St. Nicholas' Day, so it's not too early to sing "Santa Claus Is Coming to Town."

 7 The Philharmonic Society of New York, the first permanent orchestra in the United States, held its first concert on this day in 1842. Despite uncomfortable seating, the event was a huge success.

 8 If you're ever in New York City's Central Park, look for the Strawberry Fields. This memorial to John Lennon was installed there after he was killed on this day in 1980.

 9 In 1881 the Chicago opera house burned to the ground. On this day eighteen years later opera star Adelina Patti sang "Home Sweet Home" to celebrate its reopening.

 10 The 1990 *Billboard* Music Awards named "... But Seriously" by Phil Collins the top worldwide album and "Nothing Compares to U" by Sinead O'Connor the top worldwide single. These were just one of several top honors won by these stars.

 11 Brenda Lee, a singing star during the early rock 'n' roll days, born 1944. She began singing at age twelve. Because she had a very mature voice, someone once spread a rumor that she was really a thirty-five-year-old midget.

DECEMBER

 **12** Dionne Warwick, a singer and a cousin of Whitney Houston, born 1941.

 13 On this day in 1928, audiences at Carnegie Hall heard the first performance of "An American in Paris." It was advertised as "a tone poem with jazz and sound effects."

 14 In 1990 opera lovers turned into couch potatoes. For four evenings, starting on this day, they watched and listened to an unabridged telecast of Richard Wagner's marathon-length opera *The Ring.*

  15 On this day in 1991, the troops in Saudi Arabia got their own news and music radio station, the Desert Shield Network. They wanted lots of rock and rap, but also patriotic numbers like "Born in the U.S.A." and lots of love songs.

 16 Composer Ludwig van Beethoven, born in Bonn, Germany, 1770.

 17 Bruce Hornsby & the Range began to head for the big time with "The Way It Is" (1986). On this day, two months later, later the group, which is headed by singer-songwriter-pianist Hornsby, won the Best New Artist Grammy Award.

 18 Antonio Stradivari, the most celebrated of all violin makers, was born in 1644 in Cremona, Italy.

DECEMBER

 19 *Dick Tracy*, the movie with one of the most popular sound tracks ever, started its dance up the video rental "best renter" list on this day in 1990.

 20 The Bangles, a band consisting of two sisters and a friend, joined the inner circle of musicians who record a song that tops all other songs. The song that did it for them on this day in 1986 was "Walk Like an Egyptian."

 21 On this day in 1921 fourteen pianists assembled on the stage of Carnegie Hall for a benefit concert. When conductor Walter Damrosch walked on stage he exclaimed, "You people don't need a conductor. You need a traffic cop."

 22 Composer Giacomo Puccini, born 1858.

 **23** In 1980 this was another week for Kool and the Gang to celebrate the success of their "Celebration." In 1990 people were snapping up novelty Christmas cards with playable versions of the Gang's biggest hit.

 24 "Amahl and the Night Visitors," the first opera composed for television, made its debut on this day in 1951. Twelve-year-old Chet Allen sang the leading part.

 25 What do Barbara Mandrell and Sissy Spacek have in common besides Christmas birthdays? Both were born in Texas, just a year apart. Sissy is famous for playing the role of the country music star Loretta Lynn in *Coalminer's Daughter*. Barbara is a major country music star.

DECEMBER

 26 On this day in 1947 the invention of the first transistor was announced.

 27 Radio City Music Hall, a combination movie palace and live theater, opened its doors on this day in 1932. It remains a showcase for many exciting musical events.

 28 In 1911 as part of its comeback from a disastrous earthquake, San Francisco established its own symphony orchestra.

 29 Pablo Casals, the first cello superstar of this century, born 1876.

 30 Bo Diddley, a unique and influential rhythm and blues and rock 'n' roll vocalist-guitarist, born 1928.

 31 Make a New Year's resolution to learn some new songs next year.

THE KIDS' WORLD

Once you have one Kids' World Almanac book . . .

The Kids' World Almanac of Records and Facts
by Margo McLoone-Basta
and Alice Siegel

The Second Kids' World Almanac of Records and Facts
by Margo McLoone-Basta and Alice Siegel

The Kids' World Almanac of Animals and Pets
by Deborah Felder

The Kids' World Almanac of Baseball
by Thomas G. Aylesworth

The Kids' World Almanac of the United States
by Thomas G. Aylesworth

The Kids' World Almanac of Transportation
by Barbara Stein

ALMANAC®

. . . you'll want to have them all!

The Kids' World Almanac of History
by Deborah Felder

The Kids' World Almanac of Music
by Elyse Sommer

Please send me . . .

QUANTITY   TOTAL

_____ **The Kids' World Almanac of Records and Facts** _____
(pb) @ $6.95 ea.

_____ **The Second Kids' World Almanac of Records and Facts** _____
(pb) @ $6.95 ea.

_____ **The Kids' World Almanac of Animals and Pets** _____
(pb) @ $6.95 ea.

_____ **The Kids' World Almanac of Baseball** (pb) @ $6.95 ea. _____

_____ **The Kids' World Almanac of the United States** _____
(pb) @ $6.95 ea.

_____ **The Kids' World Almanac of Transportation** _____
(pb) @ $6.95 ea.

_____ **The Kids' World Almanac of History** (pb) @ 6.95 ea. _____

_____ **The Kids' World Almanac of Music** (pb) @ $7.95 ea. _____

Subtotal _____

Plus $1.50 per book shipping _____

Total _____

Name_____

Address_____

City_____ State_____ Zip_____

Please enclose a check or money order payable to PHAROS BOOKS for
the total amount and return it to: Pharos Books, 200 Park Avenue, New
York, NY 10166